HENRY KING AND
THE SEVENTEENTH CENTURY

HENRY KING

&

The Seventeenth Century

By

RONALD BERMAN

1964

CHATTO & WINDUS

LONDON

Published by
Chatto and Windus Ltd
42 William IV Street
London W.C. 2

*

Clarke, Irwin and Co. Ltd
Toronto

Printed in Great Britain by
T. and A. Constable Ltd
Hopetoun Street
Edinburgh

64 - 2554

CONTENTS

For Jean and Julius

PREFACE

THE reasons for reading Henry King are simply stated: he wrote
intellectually demanding verse of high quality, and he was actively
engaged in the formidable historical process called the seventeenth
century. One is strongly advised to use some sort of term like
'representative figure' to describe King, because we see in his ideas
some of the typical problems – and solutions – of that century. In
considering his literary course we become aware that he illuminates
those cloudy abstractions, 'the literary milieu', and 'the conditions of
the time', for he was himself part of the matrix of the century. He
accepted in his youth the literary dogmas of the Jacobean period and
wrote verse and prose of a witty, ambiguous, and complex kind. In
the time of the Civil War he began to perceive the need for a more
democratic rhetoric, and, by the Restoration, he was writing for the
most part in the lucid, simple style of the new literary generation.
His sermons and poems do not embody the brilliant, final formula-
tions of literary doctrine of Dryden or Tillotson, but they indicate,
if nothing else, the strength of will of the greater literary movement,
dedicated to a metamorphosis of its own form.

While his literary mode changed with the sensibility of the
century, his principles remained obstinately constant to the Jacobean
ideal. As Bishop of Chichester, toward the end of his long and
embattled life, he sardonically remarked: 'Chymists will tell you,
nothing can make Gold but the Great Elixar which Turns all it
Toucheth. Doubtlesse the Peoples Power is a Metall of too low, and
Coarse Allay to produce a Crown'. This plainly reaffirmed his faith
in a political and religious orthodoxy which had survived both
sectarian and parliamentarian upheavals. King was anything but a
time-server in his social convictions, and he persisted in his belief in a
society founded upon divine right when it was decidedly uncomfortable to do so. Thus, while his literary style was fluid and un-
committed, his philosophical ideas refused to recognize the passage
of time, and he preached in the court of Charles II the dogmas of
James I.

The contrast between his ideological conservatism and his
aesthetic 'liberalism' may seem inexplicable. Yet it may be said that

his literary ideas changed because his principles did not; for he was conscious of the need to give his thought as much currency as was possible in the society at large. There was no better way to accomplish this than to adopt a rhetoric with highly social implications, which would reflect his belief that the method of persuasion which reaches the greatest number with the most essential ideas is beyond doubt the most useful. It was not easy, however, for him to relinquish entirely the Jacobean mode of rhetoric. As he tried to balance conservative – really reactionary – ideas with a simplified 'democratic' rhetoric, he tried also, in both verse and prose, to keep some kind of contact with Metaphysical complexity. Fluid and democratic in one attitude, resistant and individual in another, he manifests some of the paradoxes of the century. His success and failure in merging the polarities supports our recognition of him as representative; for the universal problem of the later seventeenth century was the lucid expression of the complex, and many of its outstanding figures were involved in the selective task of assimilating the traditional into the newer ideals of literature.

Thanks are due to the libraries, the Bodleian, the British Museum and the Sterling Memorial at Yale, for their cooperation in making available the books and manuscripts of Bishop King. I am grateful also to the Office of Archives of the city of Chichester, and to the library of Winchester Cathedral. I owe special thanks to Mr Jeffrey Hart, Miss Margaret Crum, Miss Vergene Leverenz, and Professor Marjorie Nicolson. Professor Maynard Mack is responsible for anything of value in the pages that follow. I owe a final debt of gratitude to John Gorham Palfrey.

Chapter I

THE MAN

HENRY KING was born in Buckinghamshire in
1592, the eldest son of Joan and John King. His
family was more than ordinarily literate; his father was
a preacher of great reputation, and his brothers and
youngest sister were generally admired for their versification. Anne King seems to have been something of
a *femme savante*. She was enthusiastically described as a
minion of the Muses by James Howell in his customarily
execrable verse.[1] Izaak Walton was much taken with her,
for he described her as 'generous and ingenious', and he
was impressed, as we must be, by the evident friendship
between Anne King and John Hales.[2] It is probably most
graceful to characterize her verse as a genteel social
acquirement.

In Henry King's poetry she is depicted as charming
and moralistic, able to chide in couplets,

> In such a Note, and with a Quill so sage,
> It Passion tunes, and calmes a Tempests rage.[3]

One of Henry's brothers, John King, was literary enough
to have left a mass of manuscripts for future scholarship,
and he was poet enough to have had his work attributed
to his brother. His poems are probably not 'atrocious', as
has been said of one, but they are evidently no better than
those of his sister.[4] All in all, while Howell seems to have
been justified in saying 'They are a choice race of brothers,
and it seems the same genius diffuseth itself also amongst
the sisters',[5] we must admit that the diffusion was not into

9

equal shares, and that Henry remained the best literary craftsman.

John King, the father of Henry, Vice-Chancellor of Oxford and Bishop of London, exemplified both the brilliance and the limitations of the Reformation. Renowned as one of the finest preachers at court, he was a favourite of James I and an intimate friend of John Donne.⁹ He was a profound believer in the validity of the Erastian state, and a devout hater of heretics, which is to say that he was willing to burn where he could not convert. These predispositions he appears to have transmitted to his poetical son. As John King seems to have been destined for the position attained by Laud, we cannot underestimate his public and personal importance.⁷

Henry King was educated at Westminster School, 'which hath sent out so many excellent Proficients in Learning to each University',⁸ and at Christ Church in Oxford. While it must have been true that 'inspiration and competition in abundance were therefore afforded King by both institutions',⁹ it seems more pertinent to note that both were, in effect, part of the Stuart Establishment, and that they were ivory-towered redoubts of royal and episcopal privilege. King's schooling therefore had a political and theological bias. For example, his later life was devoted to the recapitulation of certain principles of Lancelot Andrewes; at the time of King's education at Westminster, Andrewes was the most popular and influential tutor at the school. Jacobean Christ Church was a hotbed of complacency. The great preoccupations of the college, it has been said, were the defense of the Establishment and place-hunting, neither of which interfered with the other.¹⁰ At the time of King's matriculation his father was Dean of Christ Church and Vice-Chancellor of Oxford. The son's close association with men like Brian Duppa, whose life epitomized Cavalier loyalty, would seem to indicate that his college exerted a good deal of influence in shaping and restricting his ideological milieu.

While King appears not to have distinguished himself academically, he did attain some reputation as a lyricist. He became part of the swarming literary life of Jacobean Oxford, writing elegies, sonnets, occasional Latin pieces, and, on one occasion, an irascible defense of his college. The occasion was the utter failure of Barton Holyday's *Technogamia*, a drama presented before the court. King acidly imputed the failure of the play to the effeminate taste of the audience, although it seems more likely that the playwright's bungling attempts at satire were the cause.

Upon taking his degrees (B.A. 1611, M.A. 1614, D.D. 1625) Henry King could, considering the circumstances of his family and the system of patronage dominant in the church, look forward to a life of ecclesiastical preferment and personal consequence. He did in fact rise rapidly, becoming Canon of St Paul's, Archdeacon of Colchester, and Chaplain to the court within a few years. His marriage to Anne Berkeley (*c.* 1617) was therefore unhindered by any wordly obstacles of the sort that beset his friend John Donne. Like Donne, King loved his wife deeply, and he lost her early. 'The Exequy', which he wrote on her death, reveals the extent of his loss. Her death, like that of Hallam, was untimely. It resulted in this poem, which seems, like Tennyson's, ultimately to repel the crude attack of criticism.

In 1621 John King died, and Donne delivered his funeral sermon. King was scarcely buried before one of those strange, murky religious scandals of the seventeenth century developed, alleging that the bishop had died a Roman Catholic. This was indignantly denied and as indignantly asserted; finally, within a year of his death, his son devoted an entire sermon to clearing his name. There seems to have been little besides popular scandal to the charge; Mason states in his life of Henry King that this allegation 'has its only suspicion of probability lent to it by the alarmed and abusive and over-elaborate denials it has evoked from all Anglican biographers and historians of this period'.[11] The son's advancement may conceivably have been delayed by his father's death, for he was made Canon of Christ Church in 1623, and it was not until 1638 that he became Dean of Rochester.

Henry King's versification coincided with the golden time of the Caroline era. At first a sonneteer, he was a willing party to the socialization of poetry, and he took his place in the world of letters as a poetic chronicler of events. With uncommon thoroughness he catalogued his age in verse, writing on such various things as the publication of Blount's *A Voyage to the Levant* (1636), Sandys' *Paraphrase Upon the Divine Poems* (1638), the death of Gustavus Adolphus (1632), and the construction of the huge warship *Soveraign* (1637). He had an observable passion for the funeral elegy; he wrote some excellent verse on the deaths of Jonson and Donne, and some considerably inferior on the deaths of various other literary and social luminaries. He may well be considered the poet of the funereal, for most of his verse is either a celebration of the dead, or of death. It should be acknowledged that, like a great many of the poetasters then flourishing, or hoping to flourish, by patronage, he commemorated the births, deaths, and progresses of the royal family, but this (perhaps) may be ascribed to patriotism.

The man who distinguished himself in the composition and delivery of a sermon then was in many respects like the man who writes a successful novel now. One's reputation was made in the literary world, at least until the next

attempt. While King was generally applauded during his
lifetime for his sermons, he seems to have begun with
something of a handicap. John Chamberlain gives a cool
but devastating account of King's first attempt; a failure
which was the more profound because of the exalted
audience and the obvious involvement of the influence of
his family:

> On Wednesday the 5th of this present . . . young King, the
> Bishop of London's eldest son, of the age of twenty-three years,
> preached at Paul's Cross. It was thought a bold part of them both,
> that so young a man should play his first *prises* in such a place and
> such a time, it being, as he professed, the *primitiae* of his vocation,
> and the first Sermon that ever he made. But this world, they say, is
> made for the presumptuous. He did reasonably well, but nothing
> extraordinary, nor near his father, being rather slow of utterance *et
> orator parum vehemens.* He hindered me from hearing the Bishop of
> Ely. . . .[12]

If King's own sermons got off to a shaky start, he was
soon to become associated with the acknowledged master
of devotional rhetoric. Possibly the most important event
in his early life was his friendship with John Donne. This
friendship was, in a sense, a heritage from John King.
When Donne, at the instigation of King James and Dr
Morton, determined to enter the church at last (1615), it
was John King who first knew of the decision, and who in
fact, ordained him:

> And declaring his intentions to his dear friend Dr *King* then
> *Bishop* of *London,* a man famous in his generation, and no stranger
> to Mr *Donne's* abilities, (for he had been Chaplain to the Lord Chan-
> cellor, at the time of Mr *Donne's* being his Lordships Secretary)
> That Reverend man did receive the news with much gladness; and,
> after some expressions of joy, and a perswasion to be constant in his
> pious purpose, he proceeded with all convenient speed to ordain him
> first *Deacon,* and then *Priest* not long after.[13]

Donne became as good a friend to the son as to the father. Walton remarks in his dedication of the life of Donne to Sir Robert Holt of Aston (King's nephew), 'And Dr *Donne's* love died not with him, but was doubled upon his Heire, your beloved Uncle, the Bishop of Chichester. . . . And this affection to him was by Dr D. so testified in his life, that he then trusted him with the very secrets of his soul'.[14]

As Walton observes, King and Donne were in daily association at St Paul's, the one as Chief Residentiary, the other as Dean. When Donne became dangerously ill a few years after his appointment as Dean, it was King who offered to ease his mind of financial worries by granting him the income of church lands within his disposal. Donne was grateful for the offer, but refused on the grounds that to accept would be to commit sacrilege, since he would be unable to justify to God a diversion of church funds for private use without value returned.

If Donne had scruples about the gift he had none about the giver. In Walton's version of Donne's speech of refusal King was a 'most *faithful friend* and Executor', of whose 'Care and Justice' Donne had no doubts. When Donne died he bequeathed some personal possessions to King, and some pictures. One of the latter was the famous winding-sheet drawing described by Walton:

> He brought with him into that place his winding-sheet in his hand, and, having put off all his cloaths, had this sheet put on him, and so tyed with knots at his head and feet, and his hands so placed, as dead bodies are usually fitted to be shrowded and put into their Coffin . . . and when the Picture was fully finished, he caused it to be set by his bed-side, where it continued, and became his hourly object till his death.[15]

After this picture King caused to be carved the statue which stands today in St Paul's. His own best commemoration of Donne was his elegy 'Upon the death of my ever desired friend Doctor Donne Dean of Pauls', a poem which, like Carew's elegy, is impressive both as versification and criticism.

There is a considerable mystery about certain manuscripts left to King by Donne. King did not publish them, and it has been conjectured that they were stolen from him by John Donne, the eldest son of the poet. Sir Edmund Gosse believed that their publication by the younger Donne is evidence of the theft, but his evidence is not conclusive. His guesswork on the entire relationship of King and Donne should be balanced by other authority.[16]

There is probably very little use in trying to establish a direct line of influence by comparing poems of one with the other, because, while King admired Donne 'on this side idolatry', he was individual enough to use Donne's general poetical mode rather than use his images and ideas as a quarry. He took from Donne a tough-minded, concise approach to poetry, a feeling for concrete imagery, and a kind of satirical criticism, and with this the idea of influence should be appeased.

The consecration of Henry King as Bishop of Chichester might have been expected to mark a fitting culmination to a typically Jacobean career, a final recognition by the court of his literary connections, his family's reputation, and his own undoubted piety. He was consecrated, however, in 1642, and by then the golden age of patronage was over. James I had been succeeded by his son, who was as politically obtuse as his father, and even less disposed to compromise. The country was humming with rebellion: King's consecration had followed the arrest of Laud and Strafford, the calling of the Long Parliament, and the Root-and-Branch petition, which urged the abolition of episcopal government. The Earl of Clarendon indicated that King's evident piety and morality determined his elevation, since it was felt that such an appointment would make the episcopate less odious to the opposition.[17] What this opposition was like, in its less lucid moments, is perhaps best viewed in William Prynne, who concluded: 'the tyranny, Lordlinesse, prophanenesse, Superstition and Innovations of our Prelates both in Ceremones, Doctrine, Worship, have been the Originall, Principall, if not onely cause of all those Sects, divisions and Separations lately sprung up in our Church'.[18] There was little chance of compromise between such opinions and the equally rigid opinions of Laud and Charles. The year 1642 marked not only the consecration of Henry King, but also the commencement of the Civil War.

The new Bishop of Chichester demonstrated that a life of literary pursuits had not necessarily disqualified him from loyal and self-sacrificing action. King manned Chichester with Royalists and took charge of its defense. His defenders, however, were not able to withstand the zealous, efficient attack of the Puritan army, and Chichester was taken in 1642 by the forces of Sir William Waller. The exposure of Chichester to victorious enthusiasm is pointedly described in a document written by King's Dean:

To this purpose, the Rebells under the Conduct of Sir *William Waller*, entering the City of *Chichester* on *Innocents day*, 1642, the next day, their first businesse was to Plunder the Cathedral Church; the Marshall therefore and some other Officers having entred the Church went unto the Vestery, there they seize upon the Vestments and ornaments of the Church, together with the Consecrated Plate, serving for the Altar, and administration of the Lords Supper: they left not so much as a Cushion for the pulpit, nor a Chalice for the Blessed Sacrament: the Commanders having in person executed the *covetous part* of Sacriledge, they leave the *destructive* and *spoyling part* to be finished by the Common Souldiers.

* * * * *

They rent the bookes in pieces, and Scatter the torne leaves all

16

over the Church, even to the covering of the Pavement, but against the Gownes and Surplesses their anger was not so hot, these were not amongst the *Anathemata*, but might be reserved to secular uses: in the South crosse Ile on the one side, the history of the Churches Foundation was very artifically pourtrayed, with the pictures of the Kings of England. . . . These Monuments they deface and mangle with their hands and swords, as high as they could reach: and to shew their love, and Zeale to the *Protestant Religion* established in the Church of *England*, one of those Miscreants picked out the eyes of King *Edward the sixt's* picture, saying, *That all this mischief came from him, when he established the booke of Common Prayer.* On the Tuesday following . . . they ran up and down the Church, with their swords drawn, defacing the Monuments of the dead, hacking and hewing the Seates, and Stalls, scratching and scraping the painted walls: Sir *William Waller*, and the rest of the Commanders standing by as spectators, and approvers of these Barbarous Impieties.[19]

This was not the only experience which drove King to a fierce personal war with the Commonwealth. With the abolition of the episcopate came also widespread sequestration; King was one of thousands of ministers dismissed and impoverished by the ecclesiastical committees of Parliament. He was stripped of his church revenues and fined beyond his resources: his library was destroyed and his personal fortune consumed, as he states in his will, by 'Publick calamitie or private iniurie suffered in these days of discention'.[20] Since King was obviously a 'Malignant' or enemy to the new government, he was afflicted even after this. He was driven out of several places of refuge, until finally sheltered by Sir Richard Hobart at Langley in Bucks. When England came under the Commonwealth government he took refuge with Lady Salter at Richings, in the midst of the 'little college' which included his sister Anne and John Hales.[21]

King was profoundly shaken by what he considered the

nihilism of the revolution. While his 'Elegy On Sir Charls Lucas, and Sir George Lisle' is a passionate enough denunciation of Puritan Machiavellianism, his two elegies on Charles I are incoherent with rage:

> Spirits-of-witch craft! quintessential guilt!
> Hels *Pyramid*! another *Babell* built!
> Monstrous in bulke! above our Fancies span!
> A *Behemoth*! a Crime *Leviathan*![22]

Contemporary poetry contained some fairly brisk digs at Puritanism, but nothing on the order of these rhymed curses. They are perhaps classical examples of the destruction of the form of expression by underlying emotional sincerity. It should be noted that it takes a fairly dedicated reader to get through these verses; the three elegies of abuse make a total of more than a thousand lines, this from a poet of sonnets. Charles I —

> An English *Salomon*, a *Constantine*;
> *Pandect* of Knowledge, Humane and Divine

—was to be the symbol for King of the destroyed civilization, and Parliament that of diabolism incarnate.

It is perhaps surprising that in 1651, from his retirement, King brought out a translation of the Psalms. Yet they are fittingly songs written in adversity. He was an intelligent critic of psalmody, as we can see in his letter to Archbishop Ussher and his poem to George Sandys (Chapter v post), but one could, I think, safely fall back on Saintsbury's characterization of his performance: 'Irritating inadequacy alike in metre and phrase'.[23] The translation, however, was enthusiastically received, and King was for many years after his death renowned as the man who had united sense and simplicity in the translation of holy song. Samuel Woodford, who translated the Psalms after King, stated that he scarcely dared compare himself with a man whose work 'must be judged meriting all Praise'.[24] Edward Phillips, William Winstanley, and others, in writing of the literary lights of the immediate past, agreed that King's *Psalmes of David* was very nearly beyond criticism.[25] One of the few judicious critics, John Patrick, anticipated Saintsbury when he stated that King's irregular meter constituted an 'unlucky method in his Translation'.[26]

King's poems came out in a pirated edition in 1657. Richard Marriot and Henry Herringman, the publishers, attached a coy preface to the *editio princeps*, addressed to the author. It was based on a kind of Baconian realism, for they claimed that the poet's delay in publication had forced them, as representatives of the public interest, to a wholesome plagiarism in the interests of art. At any rate, King now had a public as well as a private poetic reputation. What this implied is perhaps best summed up by the adulation of Payne Fisher: ' 'Tis evidently known, my Lord, that you have not onely a profound Judgement, but also a sublime Genius in Poetical Compositions'.[27] The literary biographers of the later seventeenth and early eighteenth centuries also applauded his 'wit and fancy', and he seemed firmly established as a pillar of the community of letters.

After some twenty years of Puritan domination (1659), at the risk of exile or execution, King became involved in a conspiracy. At the instigation of the Earl of Clarendon, who was then safely in France, King and his friend Brian Duppa, Bishop of Oxford, organized a clandestine apparatus for the consecration of new bishops.[28] The bishops then alive were so old or infirm that if the Puritan rule lasted much longer, the order could no longer be perpetuated. The possibilities, in an order based on hierarchy, varied from the ridiculous to the tragical. The government became aware of King's 'plot' and sent searching parties to Duppa's household for incriminating evidence. Since there had been two sanguinary Cavalier uprisings in the previous year the chances were excellent that punishment would have been summary. The conspiracy was dissolved, but, to the great surprise of nearly everyone, the Cromwellian government collapsed, relieving the anxious churchmen from the necessity of again attempting to carry out the dangerous 'laying-on of hands'.

With the Restoration King resumed the See of Chichester, and began his vigorous rhetorical retribution on Puritanism. His sermons delivered at court refused to acknowledge the passage of time, and he repeated the Jacobean ideology of church and state with the sincere conviction that it could apply to the England of Charles II. His prose capabilities had certainly not deteriorated with age, and his adaptation of the new principles of literary 'nakedness' was, on the whole, a happy one.

These sermons were not entirely popular. The court must have recognized the laughable disparity between the ideal, biblical patriarch of the sermons and the libertine who listened to them. The ideas of divine right and despotic privilege were no longer burning issues, but by now mere anachronisms. Pepys' generally hostile comments on King should be taken, I think, as fairly representative: 'The Bishop of Chichester preached before the King, and made a great flattering sermon, which I did not like that Clergy should meddle with matters of state'.[29] King's cause was no longer that of society, and his unyielding defense of Jacobean principles could only endanger the delicately established moderation of the time. Since political obtrusiveness was no longer in style, King's bias in favor of a reactionary polity kept him more or less hermetically sealed in Chichester, while more tractable men climbed in the hierarchy.

At Chichester he tried to cope with the problems left by the Revolution. We can see some of them delineated in the following tragi-comic extract:

In the parish of Wivelsfield the tithes belonged to a Mr More, of Morehouse, to whose ancestors they had been appropriated on the dissolution of Lewes Priory. A long correspondence has been preserved which passed between Mr More and Bishop King, in the first year after the Restoration, and it affords a curious insight into the condition of the parish during the Commonwealth. The parishioners had complained that Mr More had recently made no allowance for a minister, according to the custom of himself and his ancestors for many years. The bishop required Mr More to 'settle an orthodox minister with a competent maintenance'. To this Mr More replies that he and his grandfather before him, 'out of the natural addiction we had to a scholar's company, and the respect we bore to a divine function, did uninterruptedly entertayne some student as companion, to whom we did not only show the civility of a gentleman, but in consideration of his office in the parish we allowed some salary, not out of necessity, but as we hoped out of charity, till the late sad times'. During the commonwealth Mr More's scholarly chaplains had been silenced in the church, and their place supplied, first by a presbyterian jack-maker and then by a drummer, while at the time of the correspondence with the bishop, it was occupied by an 'unlearned and unordayned maltman'. The people had endeavoured, Mr More says, 'to force me to mayntayn the maultman by giving him over all the tithes, whom I judged worthy of none'; and in conclusion he states that he is ready to 'entertayn a minister as formerly, allowing him a noble salary, on condition that he be of my own selection without stint or limitation, subject to the approval of yr. lordship'.[30]

The correspondence mentioned has unfortunately gone to earth once more.

Puritanism in the parishes of England was rather more stubborn than in London, and while the great city surrendered to a new complacency, the hinterland still enjoyed its rectitude. Pepys notes in his entry of March 25-26 of 1664 that the countryside had not forgotten fundamentalist integrity, at least according to Dr Creighton, who preached at Court: 'He said the greatest part of the lay magistrates in England were Puritans, and would not do justice; and the Bishopps, their powers were so taken away and lessened, that they could not exercise the power they ought'. Wood, in his abbreviated life of King, acknowledges that Sussex was not without its share of the obstinately righteous, which perhaps accounts for King's ardent desire to escape, via translation and advancement, to a more sympathetic environment. King's letter to Gilbert Sheldon, Archbishop of Canterbury, dated February 21, 1666, complains bitterly of the 'fanatics' in Chichester and throughout the diocese.[31] In a rather sad letter of his own, the expectant Rector of Broadwater, Dr Edward Burton, indicates that King wished seriously to leave for greener pastures:

I find they have made me Bishop of Chichester in the country, but not at court; for Dr King, our bishop that now is, was designed to be Archbishop of York; and the same was stronge, both in court and city, for a fortnight. He treated with diverse noblemen and gentlemen about renewing of leases, and with the two chaplains to goe with him into the North. The Bishop told me himselfe he was to remove, hearing that I was to be his successor; and, after all this, he withdrew himselfe into the country, and, through his negligence and carelessness in not following it up as he ought to have done, Dr Frewen, the Bishop of Coventry and Litchfield, got it from him, and by this means he continues here, to his losse and my prejudice. I should have had very good preferment in another county, but being old, I only desire it in my own. . . . Edward Burton.[32]

For the remaining few years of his life however, King seems to have been condemned to a purgatory of sectarian irritations. He escaped only occasionally by preaching in

London. King's last sermons, intensely dissatisfied with moderation, and heroically intemperate against Puritanism, perhaps reflect this final disappointment: The Resurrection had come, yet mankind still defied salvation.

King died in 1669, his life having spanned the period between Elizabeth and Charles II, between Donne and Dryden. He left behind him myriads of testimonials on his piety and artistry. His contemporaries thought of him as a figure of real consequence as poet and translator, and Fuller's lines in *The Worthies of England*, 'his printed sermons on the Lord's Prayer, and others which he preached, remaining fresh in the minds of his auditors, will report him to all posterity',[33] began a tradition of his excellence in the sermon which was perpetuated for two centuries. In general the eighteenth century confirmed contemporary opinions on his piety, and ignored his savage philosophical and satirical attacks on Puritanism (although the latter might well have tended to demonstrate the authenticity of his piety). His secular poetry was ignored, while a good deal of lip-service was paid to the competence of his sermons. Since nearly all of the comments on his sermons, made by men like Wood, Winstanley, and Giles Jacob were identical in content and phrasing, it would seem that their 'criticism' was itself an act of religious and literary piety.[34]

By the time the great literary historians of the period, Johnson and Warton, had compiled their works, King had become obscure. He is not discussed in the *Lives of the Poets* or in *The History of English Poetry*. In the age of Johnsonian criticism, when Donne's works could be described as, 'fraught . . . with false thoughts, affected phrases, and unnatural conceits',[35] the work of even so transformed a Metaphysical as King was not accepted. Even in the nineteenth century King's respectability was praised at the expense of his artistry. The terribly limited selection of his works in anthologies indicates that the sensibility of the world of *belles lettres* was centered on pretty images and mournful thoughts. That viewpoint which preferred work 'glowing with poetical beauties'[36] was paramount. Luckily, some of King's works were of the sort that glowed 'with poetical beauties', and he continued to be read, if not understood.

Modern scholarship on King began in 1843, when the Reverend J. Hannah brought out a remarkable volume of King's poetry. This book, with its wealth of biographical and editorial information, became the basis for all future work on King. In the twentieth century, King, in a small way, had a renaissance along with Metaphysical poetry. Anthologies presented larger selections of his poetry. Between 1914 and 1925 three complete editions of his poems were published.[37] T. S. Eliot, as usual, was one of the first to see the importance of King. 'The Metaphysical Poets' praised King's ability to deal with death in the manner of Donne, and first expressed the opinion that his poem 'The Exequy' was one of the great seventeenth-century elegies. Since then there have been scattered references to King in critical works. He is at present barely within the periphery of familiar poets.

It is, I hope, clear that even so short a description of King raises certain questions. For one thing, his religious poetry is unexpectedly unlike that of Donne, Herbert, Vaughan, and other Metaphysicals with whom he has often been associated. In what tradition then, of devotional poetry, can he be placed? His sermons have been praised times without number for their piety, yet why are they highly allusive and complex at one moment, and utterly perspicuous and unpretentious at another? What of his poetry? In the seventeenth century it seemed to be 'ingenious', in the eighteenth 'extravagant', and in the nineteenth 'pathetic'. Can we know it any better by examining it in terms of traditions and genres?

Finally, what are we to make of his philosophy? We are accustomed to live unbound by principles, part of a blind, amoebic movement of culture. But the seventeenth-century intellectual could not afford this luxury, for the act of belief was the act of life. If we think of Laud or Falkland, we may see that the act of believing transcended the act of living. The Bishop of Chichester had this kind of will; he saw in the Book of Kings the eternal pattern of human government, and the years of war, of refuge, and finally, of neglect, never weakened his conviction. Ideological resistance is something outside of our experience: the study of Henry King may have its final value as a study of a forgotten morality.

Chapter 2

HENRY KING AND HIS MILIEU

ENOUGH has been written of the earlier seventeenth century for us to have a clear idea of its philosophical dialectic. It is therefore not the purpose of this chapter to rewrite an intellectual history of the time, but to examine what was probably the immediate intellectual milieu of Henry King. In the works of three men who were closely associated with him and who covered the spectrum of Anglican thought, John King, John Donne, and John Hales, we seem to find a good deal which bears on his own position. The comparison of John King, Bishop of London,[1] and his son seems to have a certain relevance, for, apart from the superficial resemblance of their careers, both followed the same course of passionate loyalty to the Stuart cause. John King set an example of rigid resistance to the new reforming movements in church and state, and of intense idealization of the monarchy. He was one of those who saw in the Stuart rule a transcendent proof of divine providence, and he became an apologist for the theological and political doctrines which were then 'official'. Like his son he rejected a passive role in the war of ideas, and he defended his beliefs by tracts, controversy, and fire. His role in one of the last executions for heresy in England is, to say the least, worth noting. Fuller is the best narrator of the trial and death of Bartholomew Legate, whose accuser and judge was the Bishop of London:

Often was he convented before the bishops in the consistory of St Paul's, where he persisted obstinate in his opinions, flatly denying the authority of that court. . . . The disputation against him was

26

principally managed by John King, bishop of London, who gravelled and utterly confuted him with that place of scripture, (John xvii. 5,) '*And now, O Father, glorify Thou Me, with Thine own self, with the glory which I had with Thee before the world was.*' This text, I say, was so seasonably alleged, so plainly expounded, so pathetically enforced by the eloquence and gravity of that bishop, (qualities wherein he excelled,) that it gave marvellous satisfaction to a multitude of people there present, that it is conceived it happily unproselyted some inclinable to his opinions; though Legate himself remained pertinacious, both against the impressions of arguments and scripture, daily multiplying his enormous opinions.

* * * * *

For maintaining these opinions, Legate had long been in prison in Newgate, yet with liberty allowed him to go abroad; not contented wherewith, he openly boasted, and often threatened to sue the court which committed him for reparations for false imprisonment; so that his own indiscretion in this kind hastened his execution.

For hereupon bishop King finally convented him in the consistory of St Paul's; and that worthy prelate, foreseeing that his proceedings herein would meet with many listening ears, prying eyes, and prating tongues, chose many reverend bishops, able divines, and learned lawyers to assist him: so that the consistory, so replenished for the time being, seemed not so much a large court as a little convocation. By the counsel and consent of these, by his definitive sentence he 'pronounced, decreed, and declared the foresaid Bartholomew Legate an obdurate, contumacious, and incorrigible heretic'; and by an instrument called a *significavit* certified the same unto the chancery, delivering him up unto the secular power. . . . Whereupon king James, with his letters dated March 11,[2] under the privy seal, gave order to the broad seal to direct the writ *de haeretico comburendo*.

* * * * *

To Smithfield he was brought to be burned. . . . Vast was the conflux of people about him. Never did a scare-fire at midnight summon more hands to quench it, than this at noon-day did eyes to behold it. At last, refusing all mercy, he was burned to ashes. And so we leave him, the first that for a long time suffered death in that manner; and O that he might be the last to deserve it.[3]

The general crime of Bartholomew Legate was that he was sectarian. His particular crimes were that, like the despised Anabaptists, he rejected the doctrine of baptism, disbelieved in the Trinity, and claimed that Christ was mortal. He did not improve his position by his persistent denial of the right of the Established Church to existence, and of its capacity to try him. He was tried for a variety of reasons: Fuller notes that James, in his character of most disputatious monarch in Christendom, took a personal interest in converting Legate. One historian remarks that, failing in this, he 'egged on ecclesiastics'[4] to Legate's conviction. The warrant for his death cited its justification in 'the manifest example of other Christians, lest they slide into the same fault'.[5] The court undoubtedly considered the trial to be an example for those vociferous 'other Christians' who might be suspected of desiring to modify or abolish the ecclesiastical polity.

John King's conduct in the Legate affair had of course ancient and honorable precedent. And Calvin's execution of Servetus had occurred within the memory of living man, an execution justified by the argument that the victim was a public danger as tangible as the plague.[6] The Protestant world, if we review the reaction to the trial, concurred in the praise of 'justice':

Melancthon declared that he had earned the gratitude not only of the whole Church but of all posterity. Haller said that Servetus had received his just reward. Musculus commended the execution in some elegant verses which he sent to his colleague Blaurer, at Basle; while Peter Martyr, in a letter to the Polish nobles, called Servetus 'a child of the devil', and said that Geneva had done its work well.[7]

John King, like Calvin, Luther, and other Christian thinkers, was intensely conscious of the Christian community. It is no accident that he considered heresy as sedition, for to attack this community at one point was to attack it in all. In a century of religious war this was treason, and execution was the most relevant form of justice.

It was in this tradition that Henry King matured. John King's defence of what he considered to be order relates not only to the earlier Protestant movement, but to the later conflict in which his son was engaged. The trial of Legate, if it accomplished nothing else, established a 'climate of opinion' in which Henry King had to live. It continued the tradition of militant religion into the church of his experience. It may be inferred that this influenced Henry King to think in categorical terms, for, while his philosophical position is on the one hand intellectual and humanistic, it is on the other uncompromisingly fundamentalist. Thus, after the Restoration, we have the anomaly of his sermons continuing the war against schism while the world lapsed gratefully into moderation. We have reversion to earlier modes in his advocacy of capital punishment for all even remotely concerned with the death of Charles I:

It is the Positive Law of God, *He who sheddeth Man's Blood, by Man shall his Blood be shed.* And I know not what Power upon Earth can dispense with it. If there be any who frame excuse, or by Sophistry and False Reason endeavour to Palliate the Crime, let them take heed lest they pluck down the Guilt upon Themselves.[8]

Whether or not this was Christian was perhaps not so important as whether it was feasible. It was simply a reversion to a mode which had recently been appropriate.

The idea of order which John King defended was part of the Anglican tradition, and, as such, was accepted by his son. This order was threatened by the nonconformists of the nation. The general cultural apprehensiveness about the direction of Puritan worship had already found a voice in Hooker, whose *Of The Laws of Ecclesiastical Polity* was the great rational defense of his church. It was Hooker's

29

contention, and certainly that of John King, that royal and episcopal authority were the means to earthly harmony. But the rejection of such authority and the increasing atomism of Puritanism were manifest. Each reading of the Bible, while vigorous and devout, brought forth new conflicting opinions. A sudden 'revelation' could create a new sect, righteously and irrevocably opposed to its milieu. Authority and individualism could not subsist together; Zeal-of-the-land-busy's declaration, 'Surely, it may be otherwise, but it is subject to construction', is perhaps what ultimately marks him as a cultural dissident. Hooker's comment on the infinity of attitudes possible to Puritanism is one of conservative mistrust: 'When they and their Bibles were alone together, what strange fantastical opinion soever at any time entered into their heads, their use was to think the Spirit taught it them. . . . it was no marvel to see them every day broach some new thing, not heard of before'.[9] The 'new thing' was to be dreaded insofar as the old order was to be maintained.

The 'new thing' was the object of John King's hostility. He followed Hooker and Andrewes, and seems to have anticipated not only his own son, but Laud and others (who were not merely High-Church but, if the term may be used, politically spiritualized) in his defense of a rational and authoritarian polity. We can see the explicit statement of his doctrine in one of his works, *The Fourth Sermon Preached at Hampton Court on Tuesday the Last of Sept. 1606*. In this sermon he expounds the unity of church and state by likening the church to a vineyard, 'planted by Gods right hand, grounded in faith, rooted in charity, watered by the word of the preachers'.[10] But this garden, like Milton's Eden, is rationally circumscribed. It is not abandoned to the rule of nature, but worked, disciplined and, in essence, formed, by its overseers. Just as, in

Paradise Lost, Adam represented a rational control over nature's luxuriance in Eden, in this garden the keeper makes the creation, in some sense, intelligible. Probably the most important thing to note is that the keeper is conceived of politically: 'The *Keepers* of this vinyard are both the *magistrat, & minister.* for that the former also is, can not be doubted: he is *nutritius ecclesiae*, the *nursing father of the Church.* . . . Kingdomes of the earth are good helps and furtherances to the kingdome of heaven.'[11] It was a truism of Renaissance theory that the '*Diademe & Ephod*' must form a unified structure: it was also true that a balance of authority was implied, and that this balance was no longer accepted fully by dissenters.

The Bishop of London is quite willing to admit that the keepers are subject to every variety of human corruption (although he sticks rather closely to Roman Catholicism for exempla), but he shows Burkeian tenacity in arguing for conservation of the structure of the church. The necessity of authority is pointed up by the Anabaptists, an ever-useful symbol for religious nihilism, objectionable alike to Catholic and Anglo-Catholic. He contends that English dissenters must eventually, like Anabaptists, come to cultural sedition, a hypothesis borne out by the history of the Puritan movement. It is worth noting that in his lengthy discourse on Puritanism he attacks his subject with scrupulous logic rather than with what were already the clichés of satire. We may infer from this sermon that King was attempting to deal intellectually with a problem that could not be fully described intellectually. It was not difficult for him to belittle the origins and privileges of the presbytery. Nor was it difficult, in the light of generally accepted Renaissance theory, for him to criticize the lese-majesty of schismatics. But he seems not to have understood that the conventicle was not the real basis of Puritanism.

His own concern with form led him to view with distaste the amorphous, democratic sectarian congregation, so that he could dispose of the new movement simply by stating of the typical adherent that he was 'to day a *tradesman*, to morrow a *churchman*, to day an *artificer*, to morrow an *elder*; & so likewise backe againe'.[12] It was of course a mistake to use criteria of form to judge phenomena of sentiment, but this was not then apparent. At any rate, Bishop King erred in failing to consider that the concentration of Puritanism upon salvation, its offer of absolute certainty in faith, constituted its most profound attraction. He misjudged its content by its form.

John King did not err in foreseeing that the new schism meant a displacement of power, even of 'Nature'. The Counter-Reformation did not contain the sole threat to traditional, 'natural' ideas of political sovereignty: Calvin, Knox, Buchanan, as well as the nameless street-corner pamphleteers of the Puritan movement, repeatedly urged that political authority lay in the priestly province. To a man educated by Tudor ideas this could only have represented a serious imbalance in the state. If there was a single fact of importance which had emerged from the rule of Elizabeth, it was that the state did not intend to become a model of the New Jerusalem, but did intend to effect a progressive compromise among its ideological elements. The tradition of autonomous monarchy could tolerate neither the political claims of the Papacy, nor the complementary theocratic ideals of Geneva, 'it being no more possible there should be two *authenticke* authorities within one kingdome, then that one and the same bodie can bear two heads'.[13] Whatever we say about 'Nature' in the Jacobean state must have reference to hierarchy, and hierarchy, of course, culminates in the rule of one. Henry King's exasperation with the claims of the many to political authority seems to derive, not only from his faith in the meaning of scripture but also from his father's preference for the unified, coherent rule of one:

> God Institutes, the People constitute the King; God gives the Kingdome, the people deliver it; God elects, but the People confirme the Election. If this be true, sure our Bibles are false, and our interpretation as erroneous as our Texts: Why doe not these Men who in many things so neerely parallel the Jesuites, get leave from their *Consistory*, as the other from the *Conclave*, to frame an *Index Expurgatorious*, to expunge those places of Scripture which make against them? Blot out that of *Daniel: The most High ruleth in the Kingdome, and giveth it to whomsoever He will.*[14]

The idea of proper authority in church and state preoccupied John King to the extent that he gave it equal importance with the search for ultimate theological truth. Coherence — 'I would in the name of God they were throughly [*sic*] perswaded, that they are as strictly bound to preserve *unum*, as *verum*, *unity* as *verity*, *pacem*, as *fidem*, the *quiet* as the *faith* of the Church'[15] — is itself proof that 'Nature' *is* being followed. Under Elizabeth this concept had served as a generally accepted justification of the religious *via media* which was not, after all, too distasteful to the conflicting ideological parties within the state. The growing conviction among the 'Opposition' however, that the will of God demanded a reformed theocratic polity, resulted in renewed application of the idea of 'Nature' by the party in power. In the face of growing religious, and by now political, zeal there was a hardening of the dogma of 'Nature'. John King and his son retreated to the position of ultimate coherence, the belief that in absolute monarchy, rigorously interpreted, lay the only solution for a besotted society.

The monarch becomes living proof of Divine Providence. Like the patriarchs ('our Salomon, our Pacificus'), he morally sustains the tribe; by exercising the ritual of government he attains a quasi-divine character. The man James becomes a point of tangency between heaven and earth, in touch, as it were, with the mundane and the will of God. Since heaven contains the principle of unity itself, it becomes only natural to expect that through this charismatic figure the natural world can hope to embody divine form. The obligation of schismatics is plainly to leave off their ephemeral speculation, and to become part of the providential scheme by incorporating themselves into the polity. This aspect of John King's theology was passed directly on to Henry King, in conjunction with the supporting theory of the Anglican tradition. Human law, for example, lay under the obligation of conforming to Divine law, so that we find, in Hooker and other apologists, a seemingly authoritarian imperative: it is 'a thing unlawful for private men, not called unto public consultation, to dispute which is the best state of civil polity'. Thus, there is no possible reason, by analogy, 'why they should better judge what kind of regiment ecclesiastical is the fittest'.[16] As Bishop Andrewes flatly stated, rebellion against the laws of the natural world was equivalent to rebellion against those of the greater world. No 'dependency, or superiority, or subordination' is against the law of reason, and a king, 'is . . . one against whom there is no rising: So God would have it'.[17] We should then be prepared to find in Henry King a preoccupation with the state of man insofar as it must reflect the form of the eternal world. When we encounter his transcendent vision of a righteous government we should recognize its affinities with the vision of the Anglican apologists:

There is nothing which more clearely demonstrates the *God of Order*, then the subordinate Government of the Kingdomes of the Earth. Nor doth any forme of Government come so neere His

Owne, which is the Archetype, the first and best patterne of all others; as the Monarchall, when a state is governed by a King as sole Commander over all. For in this singularity of power, that person who is ... the lively Image of God, will some way represent the Unity of his Maker too. ... And He who kindled that Glorious light in the Firmament, *Set up also the King* to governe by the splendour of his Authority upon Earth; as being *the Light of our Israel*, and Gods Lieutenant; or (so *Plato* calls Him) as God amongst Men.[18]

If this passionate belief in unity depended ultimately upon a synthesis of parts of the Book of Kings and the *Republic*, it came to Henry King through the immediate agency of John King, Bishop of London.

In John Donne we find another possible source for Henry King's position. It is not beyond reason to suspect that the similarities in their philosophy bespeak not only a common tradition but the shared ideas of years of friendship. While we find in King much more concern with the relationship of religion to the structure of society than is to be found in Donne, we see that Donne too is alive to the challenge of dissent. We may never know the precise etiology of their mutual 'influence', but we can see that, on the question of the latest Christian schism, their opinions sustain each other. While anything said about Donne's attitude towards the new sectarianism represents a scattering of opinion rather than a cohesive scheme of criticism, there appear to be three consistent points which he felt forced to defend against the 'new thing'. These were, the universality of religion, the redemption of mankind, and the need for joy of the spirit.

There was a firm opposition between Donne's relativistic tolerance and Puritanism's absolutist rigor. Donne, like King, saw in the severely uncompromising attitude of Puritanism (whether in interpreting scripture or judging society) an excess of enthusiasm. Puritanism had demonstrated early that intransigence which most perfectionist sects seem to be born with. It evidently owed its successes to this characteristic, as it did its failures. For Puritanism, any kind of *via media* was a compromise with evil. To be relativistic was to outrage righteousness, for their truth was of an excluding and necessitarian kind. Admittedly this is generalizing to an almost unwarranted extent, since not all forms of Puritanism could be so described. What is important, however, is that Puritanism represented this to Donne. If he did not see it as actually pharisaical, he did see it as fanatical, certainly as destructive of the love of God in its quest for the justice of God. It represented a striving for eternal verity upon earth, and Donne held that eternal verity lies not in the practice of one or another doctrine, but in the end towards which all doctrine strives: 'So Synagogue and Church is the same thing, and of the Church, *Roman* and *Reformed*, and all other distinctions of place, Discipline or Person, but one Church, journying to one *Hierusalem*, and directed by one guide, Christ Jesus'.[19] He rebukes the 'severe and unrectified Zeal' of those who torture 'every degree, and minute and scruple' of circumstances in order to grind from them a rigorous conclusion:

God in his eternall & ever-present omniscience, foreseeing that his universal, Christian, Catholick Church, imaged, and conceived, and begotten by him in his eternall decree . . . should in her latter Age suffer many convulsions, distractions, rents, schisms, and wounds, by the severe and unrectified Zeal of many, who should impose necessity upon indifferent things, and oblige all the World to one precise forme of exterior worship, and Ecclasiastick policie; averring that every degree, and minute and scruple of all circumstances which may be admitted in either beleif [*sic*] or practice, is certainly constantly, expressly, and obligatorily exhibited in the Scriptures; and that Grace, and Salvation is in this unity and no where else; his Wisdome was mercifully pleas'd, that those particular

Churches, devout parts of the Universall . . . should . . . be provided of an argument, *That an unity and consonance in things not essentiall, is not so necessarily requisite as is imagined.*[20]

King shared Donne's hostility to exaggerated scruples, because they signified to him a profound cultural recalcitrance. We may see that, like Donne, he mistrusts the motives of religious literalism: 'It was an old complaint, that ill Glosses corrupted Good Lawes. Those perversions have long since crept into the Booke of God, and mens particular interests have distorted the Texts there to their own practises'.[21] Even in his early life, as his sermon of 1621 indicates, he hated the Puritan tendency to 'torment a Text'. This seemed to be a consistent aspect of pertinacious enthusiasm; as Donne and King saw it, and perhaps as it existed, there seemed no detail too small for zeal to exercise its rigor. That there was a certain justice in their suspicions is perhaps evident on reading John Elliott's axiom, that Puritans should account 'no law, statute or judgement valid than it floweth or appeareth to arise from the Word of God'.[22] Donne's antipathy to this kind of intellectual absolutism was taken up not only by King, but by Chillingworth, whose *Religion of Protestants* is based squarely upon the assumption that no one way to God is infallible.

Donne gives us in his Sermons an instance – really a parable – of 'severe and unrectified Zeal'. He describes an encounter with an Anabaptist household in which righteousness manages to prevail over devotion. It should be remembered that Anabaptists were always hyperbolically enthusiastic: they had messianic pretensions, and were distinguished by such fanatical phenomena as convulsions and wholesale revelation. What is perhaps most important to note is that Anabaptism was invoked as symbolic of the Puritan movement by its enemies, so that reference to it, however oblique, is often a reference to English sectarianism:

> Lying at *Aix*, at *Aquisgrane*, a well known Town in *Germany*, and fixing there some time, for the benefit of those *Baths*, I found my self in a house, which was divided into many families, and indeed so large as it might have been a little Parish, or, at least, a great lim of a great one; But it was of no Parish: for when I ask'd who lay over my head, they told me a family of *Anabaptists*; And who over theirs? Another family of *Anabaptists*; and another family of *Anabaptists* over theirs; and the whole house, was a nest of these boxes; severall artificers; all *Anabaptists*; I ask'd in what room they met, for the exercise of their Religion; I was told they never met: for, though they were all *Anabaptists*, yet for some collaterall differences, they detested one another, and, though many of them, were near in bloud, and alliance to one another, yet the son would excommunicate the father, in the room above him, and the Nephew the Uncle. . . . And I began to think, how many roofs, how many floores of separation, were made between God and my prayers in that house.[23]

When the concept of redemption was examined by Donne, he again resisted absolutism, whether Catholic or Puritan. He was particularly opposed to contemporary interpretations of predestination. Despite the fact that this doctrine had been angrily criticized by leading Anglicans, and had been forbidden as a subject for sermons by James, it had a powerful and constant influence. Donne set himself against that most orthodox Calvinism which had established an unqualified distinction between the saved and the damned. (In later years Puritans were to insist that all men could qualify for grace because of the Atonement; in the early years of the century however, the bleak prospect of damnation was all that was held out for those not of the elect.) Predestination set the society of the damned apart from that of the saints, it gave a positive delineation to human expectations, and it justified the diffuse hostility so noticeable in Puritanism to established religious forms. It was well said by John Downame in his *Christian Warfare* (the title is an excellent clue to the new cultural position of Puritanism) that 'Whosoever therefore are predestinate to salvation, they also are effectuallie called, that is, *separate from the world*'. [Italics mine.] We know how John King looked on those who imposed their 'scruples' on the world of order he wished to maintain. Donne and Henry King were no less aware that a strict insistence on the separate worlds of the saved and the damned would lead to an earthly society forever beyond the magical unity of 'order'. William Haller, in his *Rise of Puritanism*, connects this theological position and its sociological consequences:

> If none were righteous, then one man was as good as another. God chose whom he would and the distinctions of this world counted for nothing. . . . If election were manifested not by outward conformity to an imposed law but by the struggle of the spirit . . . there could be no fear concerning the issue of life's ordeal. . . . The triumph of the saints was foreordained. Therefore nothing they could desire was impossible for them to attain. Heaven was theirs already, *and if presently they demanded possession of the earth as well, that was no more than human.* [Italics mine.]

In addition, we must remember that King was a part of a church which has often had the term *via media* applied to it. If, as a philosopher, King found little to admire in a doctrine that would assuredly destroy his ideals of civil order, as an Anglican churchman under the influence of John Donne he was spiritually repelled by a belief that, in Downame's words, 'whosoever are not called, justified and sanctified, shall never be saved'. The rigorists of Puritanism found this idea acceptable, even satisfying, but Donne and King could on this point say with John Hales a fervent 'good-night to John Calvin'. The first principle of

39

John Donne's belief was that the *agape* of God was the mark of His being. The most important event that had occurred in the Puritan theology had been the Fall; for Donne, the Atonement was the most significant Christian experience. His works consciously match mercy against justice: 'For God delights not so much in the exercise of his *Power*, as of his *Mercy* and *Justice* . . . For *Mercy* is his *Paradise* and garden, in which he descends to walk and converse with man. . . . Even at first God intimated how unwillingly he is drawn to execute *Justice* upon transgressors'.[24] He summed up his philosophy simply in another writing, 'God did not make that fire for us, but much less did he make us for that fire; make us to damne us, God forbid'.[25] As for the exponents of that uncharitable doctrine, their rigor has led them only to hybris:

Wee are fallen upon such times too, as that men doe not thinke themselves Christians, except they can tell what God meant to doe with them before he meant they should bee Christians; for we can be intended to be Christians, but from Christ; and wee must needs seek a Predestination, without any relation to Christ; a decree in God for salvation, and damnation, before any decree for the reparation of mankind, by Christ. Every Common-placer will adventure to teach, and every artificer will pretend to understand the purpose, yea, and the order too, and method of Gods eternall and unrevealed decree.[26]

Henry King also insisted that predestination was by no means the irrefutable process ascribed by Puritanism to divine Providence. He believed, as Donne did, that the zealous ignorant were attempting to impose their own will on 'Gods eternall and unrevealed decree'. Donne's 'Common-placer' is the subject of King's reflection:

You shall have a sort of Lay Mechanicke Presbiters of both Sexes . . . presume so far upon their acquaintance with the Pulpit, that they will venter upon an Exposition, or undertake to manage a

long unweildy [*sic*] prayer conceived on the sudden, though not so
suddenly uttered; nay, they are so desperate, they will torment a
Text, and in their resty Conventicles teach as boldly, as if they were
as well able to become Iourneymen to the Pulpit, as to their owne
Trades.[27]

In a later sermon, King insisted that predestination failed
to comprehend the will of God, and that it was in reality the
product of morbid imagination. In praising Charles I he
states,

> Witnesse that *Declaration* of his Majesty which banish'd those
> abstruse controversies concerning Gods Decrees of *Election* or
> *Reprobation* from the Pulpit. Themes, which onely filled the
> Hearers with scruples, and sent them home with feares; Teaching
> by it busie men to preach Christ as they ought, not Themselves,
> by venting their dangerous wit or Spleen.[28]

He shared Donne's fervent belief that not only the elect,
but all men could, by prayer and piety, ascend to God. In
one of his sermons on prayer we see a good deal of the
passionate conviction of Donne:

> It is our scaling Ladder, *Oratio iusti penetrat nubes*, our Engine of
> Battery, by which Heaven is besieged and *suffers violence* (as Christ
> said.) 'Tis our Weapon with which we wound our enemies, nay,
> *Telum est quo vulneramus cor Dei*; with it even God himselfe is
> wounded, as the Spouse in the *Canticles* cryes, *Charitate vulneror*.
> It is a thing so strong and potent that it prevails with (though not
> against) the Almighty. . . . This wrestles with God, as *Iacob* with
> the Angell, and will not part without a blessing won from Him.[29]

As for joy of the spirit, Fuller notes, 'Indeed, Predestination solidly and soberly handled, is an antidote
against despair. But, as many ignorant preachers ordered
it, the cordial was turned into a poison'.[30] What Donne
called the 'diffidence' of schismatics we should identify as
the characteristic despair of enthusiasm. It is perhaps a
natural consequence of a belief in universal depravity.
There is a manic-depressive aspect of enthusiasm; the

ecstasy which is born of confidence of election, or of illuminism, often gives way to the most massive sense of guilt. Certain Puritan diaries which have come down to us carry a myriad of anxieties like those of Bunyan, harrowing doubts and fears about the unworthiness of the self, which must be confronted on every level of volition. There is perhaps no need of going further than *Grace Abounding* to see this. The heart of 'diffidence' is the bitter questioning of the self in order to accord with the Spirit; even the elect had to face the consequences of positing a state of man utterly without the ability to help create a state of grace.

Donne opposes Christian joy to this aspect of sectarianism. He points out that the religion which makes man despair of God's mercy, and condemns most of the world as evil, is essentially useless as a support of life. He perhaps anticipates William James: 'If theological ideas prove to have a value for concrete life, they will be true, for pragmatism, in the sense of being good for so much'. If man is God's favored creation, indeed, his very son, then he should rejoice in the gift of life:

> I would always raise your hearts and dilate your hearts, to a holy Joy, to a joy in the Holy Ghost. . . . For, God hath not onely let loose into the world a new spirituall disease; which is, an equality, and an indifferency, which religion our children, or our servants, or our companions professe . . . but Goth hath accompanied, and complicated almost all our bodily diseases of these times, with an extraordinary sadnesse, a predominant melancholy, a faintnesse of heart, a chearlesnesse, a joylesnesse of spirit, and therefore I return often to this endeavor of raising your hearts . . . for *Under the shadow of his wings*, you may, you should *rejoyce*.[31]

King's simple opposition to the 'new spirituall disease' was a profound confidence in the spiritualized polity. Like Donne, he had faith in God, whose '*Arme is stretched out still*, ready to embrace . . . The Children from farre'.[32] Like his own father, he believed that in a polity which was itself a model of divine wisdom there could be no occasion for 'spirituall disease' or 'diffidence'. The works of King are permeated with his conviction that this polity allows as absolute a good life as is possible on earth, and prepares man for Paradise. He thus rejects Puritan pessimism not only because 'his Mercies . . . are Patternes by which Hee is often pleased to worke', but because the hand of divine Providence is so plainly visible in the earthly kingdom that it would be folly to despair.

I would sum up the relationship of Donne and King in this way: Donne forces himself away from meditation to confront what he believes menaces the soul of man, if not his society as well. He finds that Puritan 'diffidence' is engendered by a belief in worldly wickedness, invoked too often and with too little occasion. He foresees the splintering tendencies of the coming theocracy, where the spirit of every man was to become every man's Spirit. The great constructive impulse was to die down to the pharisaical self-assurance of the Reverend Mr Chadband at least as often as it was to ascend to a Fox or Wesley. Henry King's position is well pointed up by Donne's. While his writings generally concentrate on the social dangers of the new schism, he is hostile also to its spiritual hardness. Like Donne, he mistrusts Puritanism's urgent impulse toward transformation and its spiritual severity. In Donne we see Puritanism guilty of a breach of that *caritas* which should sustain the individual: in Henry King we shall see it as guilty of destroying the Christian community by rebellion against the manifest will of God.

In his letter to Walton, King described John Hales as 'the best Critick of our later time'. The 'Ever-Memorable' Hales was both acute and industrious, a man, 'of as great a sharpness, quickness, and subtility of wit, as ever this or perhaps any nation bred. His industry did strive, if it were possible, to equal the largeness of his capacity, whereby he became as great a master of polite, various, and universal learning, as ever conversed with books'.[33] Educated at Oxford, he distinguished himself as lecturer in Greek. Hales's intellectual parts however, were not restricted to the uses of the academy. He attended the Synod of Dort (1618) where he learned to evaluate theological disputation, and human motivation. His letters to his patron, Sir Dudley Carleton, reveal Hales's dry awareness of the modes by which a religious party carries a cause toward orthodoxy. Hales was a close friend, too, of men involved in the business of their civilization. He was an intimate of Wotton, an advisor to Chillingworth, and a trusted friend and critic of Falkland. His intellect pleased Laud, if his ideas did not, and after a rebuke because of his liberal ecclesiastical theory, he was appointed Canon of Windsor by the Archbishop. After the onset of the Civil War Hales joined the 'little college' at Richings, which included Anne Howe and her brother Henry King. He served as chaplain to this group, and, presumably, as a mild and charitable restraint upon the choleric Bishop of Chichester.

Ideas of order underpropped the theories of John Hales as they did those of John King. It was in a different sense, however, that Hales interpreted them. He valued intellectual rather than political coherence, and concerned himself therefore not with the Erastian paraphernalia of the High-Church party, but with what seemed to him to be of sole importance, the intelligent practice of piety. If Laudian political theology failed to attract him, the illogic of the sectarian movement doubly repelled him. Puritan fixation on matters of ritual, ecclesiastical administration, and theological rigor was no less unyielding than that of the Laudians; its revolutionary bias and peculiar egoism made it even more distasteful. Hales shared with Anglican apologists, therefore, a profound mistrust of the reforming movement.

The man who today appeals to the ambiguity of 'history' to reinforce his prejudices might well have appealed to the ambiguity of scripture in Jacobean times. Such reliance was, of course, perfectly respectable, for the great Anglican divines went to the Book of Kings and to Romans 13 for political justification, and the great Puritan divines hunted throughout the Bible for allusions to the New Jerusalem. Neither group, however, was prepared to admit that the opposition could see any further than its nose in interpreting the great work, and each rested satisfied that it had somehow exhausted scriptural validity. While Hales did not approve of any kind of text-hunting to substantiate dogma, he was particularly disturbed by the incredible spiritual pedantry of the sectarians. He sided with Henry King and other orthodox theologians in the great battle of the Bible.

The 'wresting of scripture' seemed to Hales to be the particular and indefensible consequence of enthusiasm. Zeal leads to fanaticism of interpretation, so that many scriptural pedants are ready to 'deal with scripture as chimics deal with natural bodies, torturing them to extract that out of them which God and nature never put in them'.[34] However latitudinarian the views of Hales were, he was committed to a communal church, so that it was perhaps natural for him to attribute to this form of enthusiasm a profound egoism: it did rest on a hyper-emancipated state of mind, a state of mind which was not likely to flourish under the discipline of a Laudian church. The dissenting bibliolater was only too likely to find in scripture the image of his own conceits. The 'greenness' of scholarship of enthusiasm, and the 'presumption' of enthusiasts could lead only to a distorted apprehension of the Word.

Probably the most profound of pedantic sins was the triumph of ignorance over intellectual humility. Schism is conceived when 'the unlearned arise and take the kingdom of heaven by violence'.[35] Like Henry King, Hales sees in enthusiasm the temper of vulgarity. King himself wrote of the new 'Holy Ignorance' that the *'Spiritus Anabaptisticus . . .* that reigns amongst many in these latter days, dares affirm. . . . Those who in our Universities and Schools study Divinity grasp onely the Dead Letter, attain not the Quickning Spirit'.[36] The anti-intellectual cast of enthusiasm particularly fosters wilful ignorance: illuminism is substituted for ratiocination, and certainly takes the place of deliberation.

To Hales, as well as to King, the letter was as important as the spirit; his delimiting position was that 'scripture is given to all, to learn: but to teach, and to interpret, only to a few'. With the scholarly aloofness of Sir Thomas Browne or Lancelot Andrewes he severs himself from any identification with popular modes of logic. His criticism of the vulgar is perhaps based on the Renaissance faith in social hierarchy then still viable in Anglicanism: he condemns the populace as the source of all the anti-intellectual and eventually anti-spiritual movements of history. Yet the Bible may be closed even to intellect: it is too obscure for our understandings ever to be fully satisfied, and to deny this is to court a particularly unthinking form of hybris. The highest of intellectual accomplishments is perhaps the admission of limitations; with this Socratic viewpoint Hales challenged what may be called the will-to-knowledge of dissent.

The great adjunct to scriptural interpretation, the

elusive and omnipresent spirit, is particularly the object of Hales's contempt. He has literally no use for the spirit-reading of the Bible, which he evidently believes is a type of ouija-board theology. Spirit-revelation was not uncommon at that time; convulsions and hysteria, as well as speaking in 'strange tongues' were phenomena accompanying the manifestation of the Word, which, depending on one's point of view, substantiated or discredited the performance. Revelation from the Holy Ghost and the ubiquitous but ill-defined 'spirit' was to be had wholesale, from Anabaptist to Quaker. Hales's attack on this phenomenon, which seems to lie behind Henry King's fulminations against 'Filthy Dreamers, Phanaticks and Enthusiasts' who abandon 'sober Reason' for the unintelligible, indicates the impassable boundary between even a liberal rational theology and an anti-rational, evangelistic theology (although it must be admitted that the latter description cannot possible apply to all of Puritanism).

Hales succinctly dismissed the bugbear of spirit-revelation with his satire:

> As for those marvellous discourses of some, framed upon presumption of the Spirit's help in private, in judging or interpreting of difficult places of scripture, I must needs confess, I have often wondered at the boldness of them. The Spirit is a thing of dark and secret operation, the manner of it none can descry.[37]

For his purposes the spirit was the Holy Ghost; all else was the product of a puerile imagination: 'He that tells you of another spirit in the church to direct you in your way, may as well tell you a tale of a puck, or a walking spirit in the churchyard'.[38]

The satire of Hales, which, after all, had both an intellectual and a class bias, failed to affect a movement with deep popular roots. In the heyday of spirit-revelation the sublime egoism of George Fox could personally appropriate the spirit with complete indifference to Halesian rationality. 'The Lord opened my mouth' is one of his favored openings to a peroration. Nothing is too minute to be interpreted as emanating literally from the spirit of God: 'When we were come quite out of the *Town*, I told *Friends*, "It was upon me from the *Lord*, that I must go *back* into the *Town* again: and if any *one* of them felt anything upon him from the *Lord*, he might follow me".'[39] Fox declared even more strongly for the illuminism which both Hales and King deprecated in the reading of scripture: 'As the *Spirit of God* was in them, that gave forth the *Scriptures*; so the same *Spirit of God* must be in all them, that come to know and understand the *Scriptures*'.[40] That this must have infuriated the Bishop of Chichester, who was still very much alive while Quakerism flourished, is fairly certain if we judge by the irritability of his sermons. The 'spirit' of course, was not unscathed by criticism in the seventeenth century. Probably the best summation of conservative contempt for the egoism of illuminism is in the works of Margaret Cavendish, Duchess of Newcastle. While present at an evangelistic meeting after the Restoration, sponsored by an acquaintance who had 'taken up' religion, she heard the following speech and its aftermath:

Dearly beloved brethren and sisters, — We are gathered together in the Lord with purity of spirit to preach his Word amongst us. We are the chosen and elect children of the Lord who have glorified spirits and sanctified souls. We have the spirit of God in us . . . we are glorified and sanctified by supernatural grace, we are a peculiar people, and the holy prophets of the Lord, to foresee foretell and declare his will and pleasure . . . but the spirit moveth me to pray and to leave off preaching wherefore let us pray.

A gentleman present, who had obviously had a sufficient dose of this provoking piety, put on a nightcap so that he passed for one of the 'brethren', and arose to make an extemporaneous speech which emptied the hall:

Dearly beloved brethren, – We are here met in a congregation together, some to teach, others to learn: but neither the teaching nor learning can be any other way but natural and according to human capacity, for we cannot be celestial whilst we are terrestrial, neither can we be glorified whilst we are mortal nor yet can we arrive to the purity of saints or angels, whilst we are subject to natural imperfections. . . . But there are some men that believe they are . . . so much filled with the Holy Ghost as to have spiritual visions, and ordinarily to have conversation with God believing God to be a common companion to their idle imaginations. But this opinion proceeds from an extraordinary self-love, self-pride, and self-ambition, as to believe they are the only fit companions for God himself . . . as to know his will and pleasure, his decrees and destinies, which indeed are not to be known, for the Creator is too mighty for a Creature to comprehend him. Wherefore let us humbly pray to what we cannot conceive.[41]

The close of Hales's sermon on scriptural abuses was anathema to the will-to-knowledge:

The Jewish Rabbins, in their comments on scripture, so oft as they met with hard and intricate texts, out of which they could not wrest themselves, were wont to shut up their discourse with this, 'Elias shall answer this doubt when he comes.' Not the Jews only, but the learned Christians of all ages have found many things in scripture, which yet expect Elias.[42]

The generosity which this implied was not likely to impress in an age of the doctrinaire, in which one of the virtues was the passion of conviction. Even Anglicanism, which fostered William Chillingworth (*The Religion of Protestants*) and Jeremy Taylor (*The Liberty of Prophesying*), stood on its own basis of scriptural interpretation and dogma. The relativism of Hales not only separated him from dissent, but placed him far to the left of the orthodox. His 'Tract Concerning Schism and Schismatics' indicates that Hales was willing to settle for a good deal less in the way of theological or political conformity than such ideologues as Henry King. The famous opening, 'Heresy and schism, as they are in common use, are two theological . . . scarecrows, which they, who uphold a party in religion, use to fright away such, as making inquiry into it, are ready to relinquish and oppose it, if it appear either erroneous or suspicious',[43] demonstrates that Hales is far less afraid of spiritual contagion than King. Heresy is no longer sedition, but a mode of thought which may have its own validity. If an ultimate intellectual coherence, a kind of montage of spiritual insights, is all that really matters, then doctrinal coherence ceases to matter. Hales can therefore afford to discard some strong Anglican opinions then current. For one thing, he is not at all involved in the theory of the divine origin of monarchy. He is willing to compromise on matters of dogma and form, if only because relativism implies uncertainty. Like Chillingworth, he might say that 'men may go to heaven by divers ways; they may all go the same way peaceably to hell'.

Inclusiveness is the characteristic of Hales's ideal church, but the Anglican as well as the Puritan parties of Jacobean England, in both ritual and theology, tended to think, not of worship, but of kinds of worship. While Henry King devoutly believed in Hales's proposition, 'now communion is the strength and ground of all society, whether sacred or civil', he was unlikely to compromise certain other ideas he held necessary to form that communion. These ideas were less concerned with being rationally judicious than with being absolutely positive. King saw within the Anglican conservative idea of unity the true Biblical Utopia, as many Puritans saw within their own theories the image of the New Jerusalem. For more dogmatic than Hales, King preferred to rely on the

ethos of party rather than on a kind of Socratic transcendence of forms. He believed, quite simply and irrevocably,
that Anglicanism was the embodiment of the will of God,
and that its structure was as irrefragable as its nature.

It may perhaps be evident that Hales's mode of reasoning ('it concerns every man sincerely to know the truth of
his own heart, and so accordingly to determine of his own
way, whatsoever the judgment of his superiors be'[44]) has a
good deal in common with that of Puritanism. Although a
corporate and even theocratic form of worship, Puritanism
rested on individual conviction. But, though the idea of
individual responsibility might be shared by Halesian and
Puritan, one would assert only a moderate opinion, waiting
for final resolution in the Elias who was to come, and the
other would insist on a rigid opinion, derived from the
infallibility of individual judgment. Ideas of 'reason',
'nature', or 'spirit' are difficult to control; the conciliatory
attitude of Hales was a product of his own character, while
the exaggerated confidence in ideas of form and methods
of reasoning were characteristics of the age.

King was not a religious individualist. In contrast to
Hales, he emerges as far more dependent on the dogma of
Anglicanism. He was not tolerant and rational, but in-
volved deeply in the Anglican mythos. He did share with
Hales some brilliantly sardonic insights into the nature of
enthusiasm, as he shared with Donne a profound mistrust
of Puritan austerity. More influential than either Donne
or Hales however, is the figure of John King, Bishop of
London, who imparted to his son an unalterable belief in
Anglicanism's divine justification.

Chapter 3

DEGREE, PRIORITY, AND PLACE

THE writings of Henry King form a theodicy of heaven and the state. His first principle is that order is the manifestation of God. Without order there could be no universe: in a very real sense, order in being is the universe:

There is nothing so much sets out the Universe as *Order*, to see how subordinate causes depend of their Superiors, and this sublunary Globe of the Celestiall. Were not this method, what could hinder a second Chaos? For in the Worlds beginning all lay in one common wombe of darkenes, it was onely order and that Method Gods *fiat* brought along, which gave distinction and visibility to things.[1]

King's confidence in the rational, ordered relationship of microcosm to cosmos is unaffected by the uncertainties of the New Learning:

Twas *He* that made this firme Masse on which we tread, laying the foundations so sure, *it cannot be moved*: Twas *He* that lighted those great Tapers in the firmament, whose successive government distinguishes our Times, our Dayes, and our Nights. . . . Tis *He that shuts up the Sea with doores*, bounding the Wave with a Banke.[2]

The description of Milton's belief, 'this beauty of order in Nature reflects the shapeliness and symmetry of the Intelligible World',[3] would appear also to be a description of King's faith in natural 'symmetry'. Regularity and intelligibility are the marks of cosmos, and should be the aspirations of the state.

For King, as for nearly every orthodox philosopher of the Renaissance, the 'perfect Diapason' occurs within the great chain of being; hierarchy is both the method and form of order. Man must subject himself politically to the will for order that the universe manifests; he must subject his will to the discipline of form. Political form is both an evidence and consequence of cosmic form, for, 'There is nothing which more clearly demonstrates the *God of Order*, then the subordinate Government of the King-domes of the Earth'.[4]

Monarchy therefore has its own sanctitude. Yet Catho-licism and Puritanism, hammer and anvil in theological dialectic, converge in an assault upon this agency of Providence. They represent, as in other matters of doc-trine, extremes of authority and nihilism: 'Whence you may plainly discerne, that these two jarring extreames, *Papacy* and *Presbytery*, whose faces stand contrary to each other, whose opinions are opposite as the sides of the Diameter, meet in this one Ecliptick line; to darken the Authority of *Gods Annointed*'.[5] For the Bishop of Chiches-ter, either extreme is oppressive. If man, like the inchoate matter of the universe, is disciplined by monarchy, which gives intelligible form to the matter of society, then its authority must be unbroken.

This is, in a sense, the preoccupation of Hobbes. That famous quarry of Anglican apologetics, the Book of Kings, yields an exemplum which even the great materialist approved: '*There was a time, when there was no King in Israel*: would you know the Character of that time? *Every man did what was good in his own eyes*'.[6] While Hobbes sees man as hyper-rational in his individualism, however, King declares that individualism is a moral disease. He has the same vision, if not obsession, as Plato; the state is a unified, spiritual edifice: 'Indeed if there be but one soule to informe the naturall body, why should there be more then one to rule the body of a State?'[7] The state too is properly called an organism (the identical imagery of infinite numbers of Tudor and Stuart apologists is one of the best evidences for the omnipresence of this conviction): 'Kingdoms and States are called Bodies, because *Metaphorically* they are so: The *King* is the *Heart*, the *Counsell* the *Braine*, the *Magistrate* the *Hand*'.[8] The rational, ordered relationships of cosmos are nowhere so evident as in the physiology of individual and state. The unity of the body, and of the body of the world, should be recapitulated in that larger body of society. And yet, *in terrorem*, within this organism there are 'distempers', perpetual reminders of divine wrath. The turbulent populace, who 'resemble the wild disorder of a wrought Sea', will always destroy the harmony of organic unity. King, no less than Hooker (and no more than Milton or Baxter), despairs of the insurgent will, the 'passions above reason', which corrupts the polity.

We know then, that cosmic unity is recapitulated on earth; that, of all forms of government, the monarchal best follows the archetypal order of the universe; and that the state is, in more than a metaphorical sense, an organism. Yet, relying once again upon the Book of Kings, the Bishop of Chichester refines upon these concepts. Unlike the materialist Hobbes or the opportunist Machiavelli, he refuses to acknowledge the validity of government unless it manifestly comes from the hand of God. Evidence for this must of course be deductive, yet it appears to be attainable through the study of scripture, if through nothing else. He examines the civilization of Israel (itself an archetype for a godly society) and concludes that monarchs were given to Israel by the Lord, that they acted as His 'Vice-Gerents' on earth, and that, most important of all, with David they became inalienable in their right. That society then, which is founded on monarchal legitimacy, is the only society with a right to existence. There is an understandable similarity to the 'official' dogma of the Stuarts. Yet King is, from the viewpoint of Renaissance logic, no less rational, and certainly no less honorable, than a more dispassionate philosopher.

The first-born of the Old Testament is inalienable in his right, the monarch in his own right:

There be but *Two Great Rights* which you find mentioned in Scripture. 1. *Jus Primogeniturae*, the *Right of Primogeniture*, 2. *Jus Regni*, the *Right to a Kingdom*.

In the first of these all Domination was originally founded; for the Elder Brother in his Tribe was *Princeps Familiae*, the *Prince of his Family*. And not Only the *Excellence of Dignity* which was his Birth-right, But the Inheritance is so fastned to Him as if God intended no separation, either by the Hatred or Affection of the Parent. . . . *He may not make the son of the Beloved First-born before the son of the Hated, which is indeed the First-born; But he shall acknowledge the son of the Hated for the First-born, by Giving him a double Portion of all that he hath, for he is the beginning of his strength, the Right of the First-born is his.*

* * * * *

The Second is *Jus Regni, the Right to a Kingdom*, which hath *Jus Divinum*, a *Divine Right* for it's [*sic*] warrant. . . . This receives such Authority from God, that the whole World cannot abrogate it.

* * * * *

But when the *Right of Succession* brings a King to his Throne, This is of all others the Noblest, the Firmest, and Carry's [*sic*] the greatest mark of Gods favour, both to the Present Prince, and to Those from whom he was Derived.

Succession to the crown of *Israel* is by God promised to *David* as one of the Richest Temporal blessings *He* could give. . . . When God is angry with a Land, he cuts off the *Line of Succession*.[9]

The alternative to a legitimate right, whether it be that of the rebellious 'Sons of Bichri' or that of a Commonwealth, is the destruction of 'order'. Rebellions are the agencies of

God's anger; they signify nothing of political or even sociological importance. Since the power to rule is irrefragable, nothing can legitimately intrude between monarch and nation. A social contract is unthinkable: Buchanan, a favorite target for King, is indicted even after the Restoration for his monstrous proposition that the governed, too, have certain inalienable rights, and even a certain parity with the ruler, in the state:

> Certainly before *Knox* and *Buchanan,* and *Junius Brutus,* These Doctrines to Diminish Princes were never broached. One tells you, the King hath no Propriety either in his Kingdome, or His Revenue. . . . Another quarrels Him for the upper-hand, scarcely grants him Precedence: If he do 'tis all, And unlesse in Private will not allow Him the Better Man. . . . Again Though the King be Greater than any Particular Subject, Yet he is Lesse then the whole People. . . . Excellent Stuff! From whence you may discern what hands lay'd the first foundation of our *High Courts of Justice.*[10]

The political implications of this idea are both magnificent and unreal. If legitimacy is the ultimate test of government there will be no restraint implied on the monarchal power. The Bishop of Chichester, not unnaturally, comes to the same king-worship as Lancelot Andrewes and Sir Robert Filmer. Ironically, he comes to share the conviction of Hobbes too, that the power of the sovereign is very nearly without qualification. The early Stuarts were only too ready to accept this as gospel; when King, in a typically absolutist attitude, orates, 'This is the *Magna Charta* for Princes, the *Great Charter* by which Kings hold the *Right* to their Kingdoms, *By Me Kings Rule*; It is *God who sets up and pulls down, Giving the Kingdome unto whom He pleaseth*',[11] we can almost hear the tumbrils roll.

It may be suspected that King was quite overcome by his charismatic vision of the monarch. He declares:

I know *Buchanan* whose study was to diminish Princes and contract their Grandeur, tells us, that a *King, though he be better and greater than any particular Subject, yet He is less than the whole Aggregate and Multitude of His Subjects*. But a Text more authentick than his tells us, in the Person of *King David, Thou art better than ten Thousands of us*, which you must not take for a confin'd number of so many, but indefinite, nay Infinite.[12]

His apology for absolute monarchy finds in every niche of philosophy some justification for his ideal. The sermons on Charles I and Charles II contain not only the conventional material of apologetics, the repeated themes of passive obedience to a king, the sin of rebellion, the saintliness of the royal 'martyr', but a positive intoxication like that of some of the more fulsome passages of *The Maid's Tragedy*. He can state that, 'we who are shrubs, and in the humble valley of a private life, shrowd our obscure heads, heare not the loud Tempests nor feele those incessant storms which beat upon the Cedar; whose exalted top raises him neerer to the lightening and rage of the upper Element'.[13] This leads to the conclusion that, 'were there no command of God, nor tie of Religion which should enjoyne us to obey and love Him whom He hath set over us, [we] might thinke ourselves bound to yield Him these duties, as largely merited in the paines he takes to support our good'. We are left, finally, with a unique mixture of scriptural and classical conviction,

When I consider the Majesty of a King, his spreading Titles, like *Nebuchadnezzars* Tree whose forehead toucht the Clouds, whose stile reaches Divinity; For God Himselfe hath said, *They are Gods*: When I consider the extent of his Command, and the subjects of His Power, I cannot but conclude with *Livy, Regnum res inter Deos hominesque pulcherrima*, A Kingdome is the most excellent thing in the eyes of God or men.[14]

The roots of this visionary philosophy are deep in the sixteenth century, yet one of its major restatements came in the surprisingly articulate works of James I, a monarch never to be sufficiently admired by the Bishop of London and his son. In *Basilikon Doron* James excoriates the 'sedition' of schism, and urges his son to remember that he holds his throne, not by the sanction of men, but by the will of God alone: God, who 'made you a man', also 'made you a little *God* to sit on his Throne'.[15] In his *Trew Law of Free Monarchies* James adds that monarchy itself 'is the trew paterne of Divinitie'.[16] He concludes with the ancient cliché that had, for Henry King, lost none of its effectiveness: 'And the proper office of a King towards his Subiects, agrees very wel with the office of the head towards the body, . . . For from the head, being the seate of Iudgement, proceedeth the care and foresight of guiding, and preventing all evill that may come to the body or any part thereof'.[17] Parliament had been sufficiently warned by James's first speech of 1603 that he intended to take rather seriously the Tudor doctrine of patriarchal absolutism: 'What God hath conioyned then, let no man separate. I am the Husband, and all the whole Isle is my lawfull Wife; I am the Head, and it is my Body; I am the Shepherd, and it is my flocke.'[18] For the time of James such a theory sufficed. Under Charles it succumbed to political realities. With Henry King, it became a valiant and visionary anachronism.

If we are to consider philosophy as existing about the polarities of pragmatism and idealism, it becomes plain to what system the Bishop of Chichester adhered. Like his father he was obsessed with form, and plainly intended the world to conform to the ideal. His answer to a revolution was a society modelled upon the kingdom of David and Solomon, a stratified microcosm of the hierarchy of the universe. He despised Puritanism because it rejected the 'form' of his culture. In contrast to the ordered hierarchy of monarch and episcopate, it offered the amorphous theocracy of the conventicle; instead of a coherent, unified body of the church, it offered, 'a Medley compounded of all Trades, of all Professions from the Soldier to the Mechanick Artizan, which in their Mixture resemble the Feet of *Nebuchadnezzar's* Image'.[19]

The disciplined intellectual form of the pulpit was outraged by the egoistical assertiveness of enthusiasm: 'You shall have a sort of Lay Mechanicke Presbiters of both Sexes . . . teach as boldly, as if they were as well able to become Iourneymen to the Pulpit, as to their owne Trades'.[20] The formal restraints of dogma and law were shattered by individualism *deraciné*: 'So many hot spirits, like Canons overcharged, recoyle against all Discipline, breake into divers factions, and with the splints of those crackt opinions doe more mischiefe then deliberation or Iustice can suddenly salve'.[21] The ultimate forms, 'Decency' and 'Order', were disintegrated by satanic demogoguery: 'They made no scruple to Preach up the Highest Rebellion in the State, & Fowlest Disorder in the Church, that any Age ever knew; Yet their umbrageous Phantasies startle now at anything of *Decency & Order*'.[22] In sum, King believed that Puritanism was animated by the spirit of destruction, and committed to political and religious nihilism. They who 'account Ignorance a mark of the Spirit', wish only, 'a liberty to profess all Religions except the Right, and exercise any Law but That which was Prescribed'.[23]

There are strange ramifications to a philosophy of form. There is no middle ground in opinion, the good is angelic, the bad satanic. King's enthusiasm was as demanding and overbearing as the enthusiasm he decried in religion. The figures of the Stuart kings are remarkable in his works for their ideal greatness. They are devout, valiant, wise beyond belief, incorruptible in their righteousness and in their patriarchal concern for their flock. These Davids in warfare and Solomons in council represent the zenith of the created world. The opposition is hardly credited with rationality. Cromwell was a 'Beast', and Milton the object of a terrible and arrogant insult:

> *Iconoclastes*, so shamelessly rails, That as St *Paul* said to *Simon Magnus*, so might I to him, *Thou art in the Gall of Bitterness*: And as the Apostle charged *Elymas* the sorcerer for *Mischief* and *perverting the Truth*; so it is very memorable This Wretch had the fate of *Elymas*, *Strook with Blindness* to his Death.[24]

The great patterns of life were the obsession of the age. Both in form and substance the sermons of Andrewes try to define life by a strict morality and logic. Laud, with his system of rites and Counter-Reformation strictness of ceremony, James, with his dogmatic ordering of the relationship of prince and subject, and Hooker, with his careful definition of the spiritual polity, exhibit in varying degrees the will to find patterns. And the will to live within these forms mattered greatly; Laud was killed for imposing too serious a ritual upon life, Bartholomew Legate for denying any ritual at all. Henry King was caught up in this striving for forms. Like Donne, he passionately believed in completely coherent universals. If this is not understood, it becomes impossible to comprehend his seemingly superstitious emphasis, as he himself admits, on 'Outward Form'. There could be no compromise between ritualism and iconoclasm. The dialectic of ideals was a dialectic of good and evil.

This deep idealizing of life in an age of remarkable mutations made it difficult to understand reality. The cosmic orientation of the Anglican-Royalist state became a remarkable imposition of ideal over fact, and Henry King was among those who accepted the myth as fact, who refused to adapt, who to the end of their lives, in the time of the Restoration, believed in the cosmic ideals of the Renaissance, and found in the *Jus Divinum* a satisfactory theory of religious and political sovereignty.

Chapter 4

WORDS OF TRUTH AND SOBERNESS

'Baroque', 'Senecan', or 'Ciceronian' are useful but equivocal categories in discussing seventeenth-century sermons. Perhaps the most important things to note are the convictions of the stylists of the time as expressed overtly in their theories, implicitly in their sermons. One of the great assumptions of the time was that the sermon was deservedly a part of the oratorical tradition. Whether in the eclectic court of James I or in the evangelistic atmosphere of the London conventicle, there was agreement about the propriety of rhetorical art in religion. It would be oversimplification, if not inaccuracy, to state that this rhetoric could be identified on denominational grounds; to believe, for instance, that the Anglican preacher was pre-eminently intellectual and the Puritan merely evangelistic. Not all Anglicans used the logical structure of Andrewes, not all Puritans preached brimstone.

The practice of the Puritan Richard Stock, celebrated by Samuel Clarke, is a condensation of those canons which governed both Anglican and Puritan, and which encouraged the complexity of Jacobean prose. Clarke states that Stock was able,

Not to expresse only, but to urge and presse too; not to confirm alone, but to commend also that that he delivered with clear method, sound proof, choice words, fit phrases, pregnant similitudes, plentifull illustrations, pretty persuasions, sweet insinuations, powerful

enforcements, allegations of antiquity, and variety of good literature.[1]

With Metaphysical *élan* the Jacobeans conceived of a
sermon rhetoric encompassing all the arts of persuasion.
That a certain redundancy was involved was not felt to be
important.

If the religious orator was responsible for the matter of
piety and its methodology, he was also responsible for the
form of its rhetoric. The literary genera of the seventeenth
century had to undergo examination on the manner of
their eloquence, an examination which seems to have
begun with the sermon, and spread to poetry. The
Restoration world of letters found, for example, that in
Donne and Andrewes 'manner' was very nearly 'manner-
ism'. Their eloquence gave place to that of Tillotson,
which was lucid, if not simplistic. Henry King was
conscious of this development of taste and style — he
probably helped to create it — and gives us in his *Sermon
Preached at Lewis* (1663) his own examination of the kinds
of rhetoric available, that which was 'clothed', and that
which was 'naked'.

King's rejection of 'clothed' rhetoric depends perhaps
on two things. There were sins of commission in religious
prose of which he could not fail to be conscious. The grand
manner of Donne had been imitated and finally carica-
tured, as the grand manner of Milton was to be debased in
the next century. And, as a devout ideologue, he preferred
to compromise his modes, rather than fail to propagate his
principles. The one thing of which we may be certain is
that he did not base his criticism on 'pure' aestheticism.

King's serious and moralistic bias is evident from his
opening remarks. He is quick to express his belief in a
rhetoric in which 'judgment' controls 'wit'. Although this
seems to have originated in Longinus, and to have died a

mock-heroic death with Dick Minim, it was taken rather seriously as a discovery in the English Renaissance. King could not originate, yet he did certainly buttress this article of literary faith.

> As Judgment is the Ballast of Wit, so Matter of Words. A Vessel at Sea, which bears more Sail than Ballast, is ever apt to over-set: so they whose Phantasie is stronger than their Religion, whose words more full of sound than devout sense, for want of just poise lose their own Adventure and endanger others.[2]

In effect, this is a rational and even pragmatic aesthetic. Like Addison, who later pointed and polished this concept, King comes to believe that the efflorescence of the 'fancy' is somehow illegitimate.

The vice of disparity between words and meaning receives short shrift from the aged and choleric critic. 'Tinkling words' may have a fine onomatopoeic effect, yet they 'but beat the air', and fail utterly in the service of the heavenly Muse. Aestheticism is carnal; the function of rhetoric must be only 'to prepare that Earth which we bear about us for final glory'. 'Rhyming cadences', 'similary words', and 'pitiful embellishments of speech', in the words of King's colleague, Robert South, merely 'embase divinity'. As King sees this affectation of the 'clothed' style, the ordering power of the rhetor was diverted to a marshalling of syllables. 'Sound' dominated 'sense'. The prevalence of words like 'perspicuous', 'plain', 'natural', 'familiar', etc., the catchwords of the Augustans, in such early writers as King and South, indicates at least that the stylistic dicta of Dryden were rather summations than revelations. 'Clothed' rhetoric was accurately defined by South as a gratuitous application of 'form' to 'matter':

> A substantial beauty, as it comes out of the hands of nature, needs neither paint nor patch; things never made to adorn, but to cover

something that would be hid. It is with expression, and the clothing of a man's conceptions, as with the clothing of a man's body. All dress and ornament supposes imperfection, as designed only to supply the body with something from without, which it wanted, but had not of its own. Gaudery is a pitiful and a mean thing, not extending further than the surface of the body.[3]

In following King, who had argued that 'flashes of un-season'd wit' must 'prophane that holy ground', the pulpit, South glorified the idea of lucidity, and indulged himself sardonically at the expense of the *dilettanti* of the pulpit – among whom he included Jeremy Taylor.

There is a political judgment implied in King's equally contemptuous dismissal of the 'naked' manner. Those who would strip a necessary complexity from rhetoric are clearly those who rebelled against all of the decorous 'forms' of culture. 'To dogmatize Nakedness' is to refuse illumination, for God comes to man through the fullness of the Word. Understanding itself becomes subservient to egoism, for these rhetorical nihilists, like the heretics against whom Jerome wrote, have only 'a rude Insolence to bear out their want of Knowledge, for Ignorance and Boldness commonly go together'.[4]

Conventicle rhetoric denies that a certain elaborateness is requisite in a sermon. It denies that a certain critical willingness must abide in the hearer, if his response is to be at all legitimate. The rhetorical complex is also *paideia*, and King flatly refuses to move from his classicist view-point. He avouches, in fact, that secular learning is no mean preparation for religious awareness:

St Paul himself . . . makes use of Human Learning, and cites some Verses out of *Epimenides*, *Aratus*, and *Menander*; which shewed, that He had studied the Greek Poets, as *Moses* the Learning of the Egyptians, and *Daniel* the Wisdom of the Caldeans . . .

supposing Religion to receive much advantage by the study of Human Learning.[5]

It may appear to be somewhat of a paradox for King to despise the zealous piety of Puritanism as incomplete, for the life of Puritanism was very nearly a ritual of prayer and sermon. Yet Puritans were, according to King, criminally indiscriminate in their piety. He is now in 1663 past seventy, at a time of life when conviction might gracefully bow to toleration, yet he reminds us somehow of the *terribilitá* of the Christ of the Gospels, that fearfully articulate, fearfully rational figure who refuses to admit that religion is intellectually passive, who insists that a right religion involves conscious renunciation of all other modes. Christianity is understanding for the Bishop of Chichester as well.

According to King, conventicle rhetoric was based on a minimum of premeditation, on powerful rather than on intelligible metaphor, and on a series of emotional crescendos. This was, of course, a commonplace of Cavalier criticism. Samuel Butler, in his poem 'Upon an Hypocritical Nonconformist' satirizes the rhetoric of enthusiasm even more acidly than King:

> But when his painful Gifts h'employs
> In holding-forth, the Virtue lies
> Not in the Letter of the Sense,
> But in the spiritual Vehemence,
> The Pow'r and Dispensation of the Voice,
> The zealous Pangs and Agonies,
> And heav'nly turnings of the Eyes;
> The Groans with which he piously destroys,
> And drowns the Nonsense in the Noise.[6]

One is very nearly persuaded that those who preached by the 'inward light' may be recognized as the forebears of today's evangelistic confidence-men.

King's own rhetorical *via media* was founded on the lucid expression of complex ideas. He has a very nearly Utilitarian prejudice for what is functional: in matters of logic, he declares that a learned simplicity is the prerequisite to the exposition of the Gospel. Like Bishop Sprat, he is convinced that the objective of discourse is the exposition of the irreducible matter of divinity: 'Though Philosophy might allow the divided Sects of Nominals and Reals, Divinity owns none but Reals; Men so sincere, and real, and material in their Discourses, That *speak Things*'.[7] To achieve these ends, there must be a delimitation of elaborate definitions and hair-splittings: 'a little Logick serves a Christian, And a man may go to Heaven without quaint Distinctions'.[8] King's friend Walton, in his life of Bishop Sanderson, praises Sanderson's sermons extravagantly, because

> There was in his Sermons no improper Rhetorick, nor such perplex'd divisions, as may be said to be like too much light, that so dazles the eyes that the sight becomes less perfect: But there was therein no want of useful matter, nor waste of words; and yet such clear distinctions as dispel'd all confus'd Notions, and made his hearers depart both wiser, and more confirm'd in vertuous resolutions.[9]

King was part of a tradition which included George Herbert, Walton, Sanderson, Sprat and others, who were very much aware that, in order to compete with the school of dissent, they must propound their interpretation of divinity with a minimum of the distractions of artifice. Yet, King was also in the tradition of the Metaphysical manner, so that his loyalty to function wavered, and his own sermons manifest a conflict between the simplistic mode and aesthetic complexity of a certain kind.

If we briefly trace the course of King's prose from early

67

to late sermons, we may perceive in him a sensitive baro-
meter to the shift of the century's sensibility. In 'Davids
Enlargement' (1625), King follows the practice of
Andrewes and attacks each phrase separately in order to
extract a precise meaning. This fragmentary style, which
he did not wholly abandon even in the time of Tillotson,
was generally considered antiquated and, by then, affected.
The terms 'natural', 'easy', or 'plain', which had their
vogue after the Civil War, could have little relevance to
such heavily intellectual analysis:

This Text hath two generall parts. The first records *Davids
Repentance*. The second, *Gods mercy* to him.
The former part containes these severall circumstances: 1 *A
resolution, I said*. 2 *The Act resolv'd upon*, Confession. *I will confesse*.
3 The *Subiect*, of that confession; *Sinnes or transgressions*. 4 Their
pluralitie, or the *Extent of his confession*; not *sinne*, but *sinnes*. A
terme implying both their generality and number. . . . 5 Their
propriety, which he assumes to himselfe; *Mea, my sinnes*. 6 He
specifies the Confessor, *unto the Lord*.[10]

King adhered to this method even in his Lewis discourse, in which he argued for less logic and fewer
'Distinctions'. Although he could not entirely relinquish
the manner of his youth, he was by no means so unyielding as Bishop John Cosin, whose mid-century
sermons were a mass of unrelieved exegesis.

This conscientious concern for the utmost precision of
thought subsisted with the sensuous, devout wit which
was the mark of Donne. In the same sermon King's vital
image of the blood of Christ undergoes a violent metamorphosis, revealing the dynamic imagination searching
for some transcendent finality of vision. The 'wide *River*
in his *side*', '*currents*', '*red Sea*', 'true *Iordan*', and 'sanguine
River' are perhaps the imagistic embodiments of that

'craving for the unattainable'[11] of Baroque art. The movement of imagery, like the movement of the antithetical logic, is remarkably fluid. King moves from point to point, from image to image, on the crest of a wave of rhetoric. Until he reaches his final statement King seems to have each image or antithesis follow the preceding as if in direct, violent imaginative reaction:

Wilt not thou confesse thy *riots*, as well as thy *Murthers?* the pollution of thy *thoughts*, as well as of thy *Actions? Christ* thy *Saviour* suffered for both; he bled for both. Though [*sic*] thy *great sinnes* opened the wide *River* in his *side*, and the *currents* in his *hands* and *feete*: thy *smallest sinnes scracht* him in the *thornes*, which he wore upon his head, or at least opened a *pore* in his *sacred Bodie*. For how knowest thou, but that, as he *bled* for thy *crimson sinnes* (as Esay calls them) through those larger wounds: so he *sweat bloud* for the sinnes of thy thoughts; that, as he suffered for *thy great offences* upon the *Crosse*, so he suffered for thy *lesser crimes* in the *Garden*: that, as he did undergoe a *publique passion* for the one; so he had an *antepassion* for the other in his *Agony*: that, as for thy foulest transgressions *he* became a *red Sea*, a true *Iordan*, a *sanguine River* the head of which streame began at *Mount Calvary*; So before his *Ascent* thither, in a lower place, not farre from the *Brooke Cedron*, he suffered his body to become a Marish, when for thy sake the bloud wept out at every Pore.[12]

The polemical *Sermon Preached at St Pauls March 27. 1640* has little of this passionate fluidity. King's style has been modified by controversy: the times perhaps now demand a more coldly serviceable manner. The characteristic of this passage is perhaps not width, but depth, not a passionate, associative logic which overleaps distinctions, but a slow rational logic which thrives upon them. Each image is meticulously placed, so that it is disciplined by the overriding idea, that of the garden. There is a judicious separation and limitation of ascription. If, in 'David's Enlargement', the mind appears to be searching rhetoric for some ultimate expression of its vision, in this sermon the mind is content to stay within the confines of the conventional, and methodically select terms and ideas from a rhetoric of a limited but accurate enough nature:

> Houses are indeed Epitomes of Kingdomes, and Gardens Models of Common-wealths. When God speaks of a *Nation or Kingdome to build and plant it*, the King is both his Over-seer and Actour. . . . His Office hath in it . . . somewhat of the dressing of a Garden or husbanding ground. Let not the Comparison seeme vile; God Himself accepts it. He is . . . (saith Christ) the Husbandman, and we . . . *His husbandry*. He sowed us in the bed of Nature, and will reape us in Glory hereafter. He plants us in our severall vocations, and by the irrigation of His grace quickens our Root, and our Leaf, our faith, and our works which are the germination and fruit of that faith. *Mary Magdalen* mistooke Christ for the gardiner, and Saint *Augustin* commends her mistake. How can we dislike the figure in his Deputy the King? when God is here pleased to expresse His Office by *Planting and plucking up by the Root*. The disorders of the people are the rubbish of a Land, their Vices like weeds; the Schismatick is a Thorne in the sides of the Church, the factious a Thistle in the State. He that desires to make a cleer and flourishing Commonwealth, must cleanse the soile from such rank weeds, extirpe the Brambles, and lop off the seare boughs, else never can any Plantation of good Morality or Religion thrive.[13]

The sermons of King's old age did not place such a staggering reliance on 'pregnant similitudes' and 'plentifull illustrations'. King reveals another profound change in his style, which is now modelled on the ideal style of the Restoration, 'despising all starchedness of set and affected speaking'.[14] He uses a sparing, lucid metaphor, shorter and less involved 'witty' concepts: 'I dare boldly affirm, upon what Clod of Earth, in what Field soever, the sharp Battels were fought, the Sparring Blows were made in the Pulpit'.[15] Or, 'think not, I beseech you, That I come to whet the Sword of Justice, or sharpen the Ax, my Office is rather to blunt it'.[16] His style is generally 'natural', if not familiar:

With sorrow must we remember the time when Old men, who needed a Staff to under prop them, Ty'd to their Swords, with feeble Knees knocking one against the other faster than the Drum beat, to shew their good will to the Cause, went tottering about the Streets: Nay, *Young Boys*, as if they had been taught to suck in Their Parents Rebellion with their Milk, march'd up and down in a war-like manner.[17]

There is little of the heavy sarcasm and hyperbolical abuse which were so frequently the only critical armament of the sermon. The stylist has resisted the temptation to annihilate with righteous, heavy-handed indignation, a temptation to which even the normally judicious Glanvill succumbed when orating on the same subject: ''Tis *Religion* to be *Humorous* and *Phantastick*, and *Conscience* to be *Turbulent*, and *Ungovernable*. . . . But alas, the *venome* of the Asp hath swoln into *deadly Tumors*; and those *seditious Principles* have shot their *poysonous* arrows into the *vitals* of the *publick Body*. . . .'[18]

While King's style developed from one polarity to another, it never became totally coherent. Some men could abandon one mode for another, but he appears to have had divided loyalties, and his self-consciously 'natural' style could not wholly assimilate Jacobean complexity. There is a dialectic of style in all of his sermons. This may take the form of a juxtaposition of a wildly metaphorical and a coldly rational manner. It is unlike the manner of Dryden or Tillotson, which is linear, which progresses evenly from one logical *locus* to another over what is essentially a road of identical rhetorical material. King inherited from the Metaphysical tradition certain lateral tendencies in rhetoric. Although capable of infinite analysis (as we see in

71

Andrewes), this style really depends on logical expansion rather than upon progression. Ideas are restated and refined by an almost endless series of metaphors and images. The mode of rhetoric may be changed in each fresh paragraph, because the mind is dynamically, passionately experiencing different modes of perception. Nor would it be too much to state that the general Jacobean tradition of 'pregnant similitudes, plentifull illustrations, pretty persuasions, sweet insinuations, powerful enforcements, allegations of antiquity, and variety of good literature', compelled a style to expand laterally.

King's strangely composite style is evident, if in a rather exaggerated form, in one of his earlier sermons. His *Sermon Preached at White-Hall in Lent. 1625* has the same structure, or lack of it, as his later sermons. The exegetical is his characteristic mode; his inescapable lateral tendency encircles every point momentarily perceived. He will hardly take his terms for granted; for example, his patient disquisition on the 'Remember' of 'Remember thy Creatour':

> Mans nature is a wondrous masterpeece of perversnesse, a mettall not to bee wrought upon by soft and easie wayes. He that thinkes by laying the obligation of a good turne upon us, to make us remember him, takes the wrong course. We are not so soone apt to forget any, as those who have done best for us, nor is there any so certain meanes to make us *Remember*, as by doing us some unkindnesse or hurt. Wee write the benefits we receive in water, they leave no tracke behinde them longer than the verie doing; but for our iniuries, wee print them in capitall letters. . . . We write them in Marble with points of Daggers for Pens, and in such Inke as *Dracoes* laws were writ in, *Bloud*.[19]

King rapidly runs through several rhetorical modes thereafter. He begins with what resembles a Johnsonian generality, which rapidly is expanded into a 'character':

It is the generall vice of Man, he loves not to bee acquainted with himselfe. . . . Like an humerous Novelist he travels other Countries, but is not able to give any account of his own: so censorious & criticall in surveying others, that he is still finding or making faults in them, but so indulgent to himselfe hee will not peruse his owne brest. . . .[20]

Rising to a higher moral and rhetorical pitch, the 'character' turns into a satire of man's 'flattery or selfe-love'. There is then a sudden break, as King turns to a ratiocinative mode, with his assertion, 'so much as I profit in the science of my selfe, so neere come I to the apprehension of my Maker'. Balanced for a moment within a rational, discursive manner, King reverts to the precise searching for words which has marked the introductory parts of his sermon:

And yet it is not sufficient onely to know him, unlesse thou knowest him the right, the best way. When the Philosopher would interpret himselfe what he meant by knowing, he does it thus, *Scire est per causam scire*, the knowledge he meant reacht as farre as the discerning of the first cause: so the knowledge of God here understood is not shallow or superficiall, only as he is in a generall consideration the cause of things, a *Creatour* at large, but in a neerer dependance, *Thy Cause, thy Creatour*.[21]

The progress of the sermon is then again altered by a series of exempla, characterizations, and amplifications in metaphor before it returns to the highly rational semantic analysis. The tendency to seize on a point and surround it by metaphor and exempla is part of the lateral, expansive impulsion. This process is repeated rhythmically. Rhetorical 'proof' is piled on 'proof'. This scheme of variation allowed the preacher a certain degree of precision and conformed to the evidently widespread contemporary demand for a multiplicity of rhetorical attacks on divinity. Such prose was naturally not very economical. Ideas and images were duplicated. Between each 'theorem' there was a string of allusion, authority, characterization, which was 'proof'. Yet the distinct advantage of this method was that the links of 'proof', those illustrations from popular characters or from recondite wit, allowed the sermon to relate more or less pure logic to the world of experience. Within each intellectual division of his sermon there is a plenitude of concentration, a feeling for the wholeness of experience. We have less forward movement than in Tillotson, but more imaginative and emotional depth.

The antithetical logic and rhetoric of the Bishop of Chichester is perhaps the key to the understanding of the changes in his manner. His later sermons, like those of Tillotson, progress in a deductive mode even while they maintain a characteristically Jacobean concentration on momentary perception. One feels a strong discipline exerted upon the luxurance of an imaginative tradition. If we examine one of King's earliest exercises in antithetical logic, we can see that ratiocinative discipline is virtually ignored. The contrast seems to exist for itself, rather than as a kind of reasoning:

Thus like a Falcon he stoopes lowest, when he meanes to soare highest, and his ambition like a bullet spit from the mouth of a Cannon, first grazes and then mounts. For behold, from these low foundations, from this flat and bottome of dissembled humility, he hath built a Tower loftier than *Babel*.[22]

A longer quotation from Glanvill also exemplifies the ability of seventeenth-century religious orators to carry on sustained imaginative insult. Both quotations represent a complementary weakness, which is a seemingly endless refinement on the antitheses of insult, to the point of stupefaction. In these cases the antithesis is meaningless, save as a framework for a tedious irony of comparison:

74

And indeed men *fought* for *Religion* till they had *destroyed* it; and *disputed* about it, till they had *lost* it. *Multiplicity* of *Opinion* had quite confounded the *simplicity* of *Life* and *Faith*; and 'twas most peoples business to *chatter* like *Pyes*, rather than to *live* like *Christians* . . . or like the *Bird* of *Paradise*, they had *Wings* to *flye* in the *Clouds* of *Imagination*, but no *Feet* to walk on the *Ground* of a *vertuous practice*. Yea, some had found the way to *swim* to *Heaven* in the *Current* of their *appetites*, and to reconcile *Covetousness*, *Rapine*, *Cruelty*, and *Spiritual Pride*, with the glorious names of the *Elect*, the *People of God*, the *Church of Christ*, and the *good Party*. . . . Thus had men got the knack to be *religious* without *religion*, and were in the way to be *saved*, without *salvation*.[23]

There are intimations of the growing clarity of King's style in the immensely interesting sermon of 1640. He makes a subtle if opinionated transition from statement to conclusion, the antithesis serving to create an aura of logical inevitability:

Indeed if there be but one soule to informe the naturall body, why should there be more then one to rule the body of a State?[24]

And He who kindled that Glorious light in the Firmament, *Set up also the King* to governe by the splendour of his Authority upon Earth.[25]

There is nothing which more clearly demonstrates the *God of Order*, then the subordinate Government of the Kingdomes of the Earth. Nor doth any forme of Government come so neere His Owne, which is the Archetype, the first and best patterne of all others; as the Monarchall.[26]

At its best, the antithetical logic seems shaped within a periodic rhetorical form designed perhaps to give full expression to the possibilities of description:

If there be (as I would hope otherwise) any such amongst us, who make such low account of mens lives, that they destroy, where they might Build hopes of amendment; or Pluck up by the Root, where they need but pare the Leafe: If there be any who in discharge of such places are governed more by Custome than Conscience, who take dark Circumstance and lame surmise for Evidence,

rashly giving *Sentence*, and as precipitately proceeding to Execution,
Let their own Soules run the fearefull hazzard of this Account.[27]

King's and Tillotson's strongest structures of antithesis
and parallelism are not merely epigrammatical or periodic,
but a balancing of concepts in a rhetoric which has a
decided logical progress. The example of Tillotson should
be glanced at:

> We are naturally inclined to evil, and the neglect of education
> puts children upon a kind of necessity of becoming what they are
> naturally inclined to be. Do but let them alone, and they will soon
> be habituated to sin and vice. And when they are once accustomed
> to do evil, they have lost their liberty and choice: they are then
> hardly capable of good counsel and instruction: or if they be patient
> to hear it, they have no power to follow it, being bound in the chains
> of their sins, and led captive by Satan at his pleasure.[28]

Of this passage we may say that 'logical progression is of
that sort; it moves by distinctions, which are antitheses'.[29]
In one of his last sermons it is evident that King also can
wind together parallel and opposition in a progressing
rhetorical period. In contrast to Tillotson we can see that
the progression from one rational *locus* to another is
slowed by a Metaphysical habit of amplification of imagery.
But he builds his paragraphs on the same idea of rhetorical
form which states, progresses, and concludes:

> The Grave is commonly as powerful an Oratour as the Pulpit,
> and by presenting the fears of an Ill Death instructs us in the Rules
> of a Good Life: My assurance, is that as the winding Sheet fits
> every Body by dilating or contracting it self to each ones size, so my
> discourse will suit it self to every Hearer. Like *Philipp's* Boy, it
> holds out to Youth a Skull, to Age, a Coffin.[30]

In the subsequent sentences King continues his blend
of parallel and opposition, which does not run the danger,
in spite of its obvious point and counterpoint, of seeming

to be artificially argued. The uncertainty of the subject, the likelihood, in fact, of life and death conspiring in such antitheses as he describes, makes his pattern of rhetoric apropos:

Who next amongst us is likely to fall into this low Centre may be doubtfull; 'Tis sure at one time or other we all must: And probably we shall not all of us a few dayes hence meet here again.

Therefore wheresoever that final Lot may chance to fall, whether on some Hearer, or on the Speaker, You will allow this Text a pious remembrancer to Those who stay behind, and an anti-dated valediction to those who next go hence. So then as St *Paul* told the *Corinthians*; *Whether it be I or You, so I Preach, and so Yee justly must believe,* That happy shall their condition be in the Next world, who after a Religious life dye well in This.[31]

Another late work, *A Sermon Preached the 30th of January at White-Hall, 1664,* anticipates the 'wit' of the Augustan age:

A liberty to profess all Religions except the Right, and exercise any Law but That which was Prescribed.[32]

In all Ages no Rebellion brake out, which had not the stamp of Religion to make it currant.[33]

The better the Persons are that attend, the greater is the honour done to the Dead.[34]

But, by his latest sermons, King's economy is not re-stricted to epigrammatic strokes. Writing, in this his last sermon, in short bursts, confining his imagery largely to quotations from the Bible, he endows his prose with an unadorned (and for that time factual) air of dispassionate objectivity. The simple statement which follows, carefully constructing a prejudiced assertion from an association of different premises, shows how far such language can go to make opinion appear to be naked truth. The logic follows a syllogistic pattern. It is taken for granted that all terms of the antithetical comparison are not only equal, but identical:

> For All are involved in the misery of this Day; In one kind or other all were Contributors unto it, Not only Those who voted in the Cursed Sentence, But Those who voted their Commission to Sit. All Those who by their Raised Forces abetted the Bloody Fact; All Those who approv'd it when it was Done; All Those who did not endeavour to hinder it, if they had Power: Lastly, All Those who do not heartily detest the Bloody Fact, and bewail the *Person* taken from us, with a lamentation worthy so Irreparable a Loss.[35]

A final contrast of two passages in the same sermon (Lewis, 1662) should indicate the progression of King's form from the rhetoric of Donne and Andrewes toward that of Dryden and Tillotson. It is perhaps needless to note that this sermon also manifests the conserving impulse which cherishes the complex Jacobean manner. In the first passage qualities of subtlety and ambiguity are marked. An idea is not only stated, but explored, amplified, and polished. In this passage, true to the formulas exemplified by Richard Stock, King attempts some kind of summation of rhetorical possibilities. The progress toward the point of logical conclusion is not of any more importance than the concentration on the varied facets of meaning of the stated idea of unity. The second passage emphasizes the progression from a premise to a conclusion. Here King begins with an abstract idea of theological argument and swiftly advances to the precise, practical deduction which his reasoning necessitates:

> It were ill Grammar, but worse Divinity, to consider Those that should be of One Spirit, knit fastest *In vinculo pacis, In the bond of peace*, whose Office is to preach a Religion consisting of Unity, *One God, One Faith, One Baptism*, as a Multitude; Or to speak unto Them, who in the Service of God's Church should go together (as *Israel* to the Battel against *Gibeah, As one man*) in the Plural: We

are met here, in *One place*, And I hope . . . *with one mind*, as the Apostles on the day of *Pentecost*; why should not I then speak to you as *One?*[36]

I grant, Disputes amongst the Learn'd are sometimes useful Triturations, which by the Flail of Argument separate Truth from Error;

But the pressing of those Arguments in the Pulpit, in Popular Congregations, oft-times suspend Religion, and make weak Apprehensions stagger from their first Conclusions.

The Reason is Evident, for when Arguments are press'd, and Objections for the Other urged, That which is most plausible sways the Hearer, and commonly carries the Cause.

Nothing therefore could more conduce to the Peace of the Church, and Confirmation of Religion, than the laying Controversies asleep, and silencing Disputes, which hang so many doubts upon the Cause, that like wrong Biasses, they draw men from the Mark.[37]

It could not be said that the latter passage actually exemplifies King's ultimate style, which is often disconnected, which is suffused, like John King's, and Archbishop Ussher's, with Latin and Greek tags, which is interspersed with 'strong lin'd' metaphor and images. It does represent, however, language of the new school of Dryden and Tillotson. Both passages, in a sense, fulfill Glanvill's dictum in 'An Essay Concerning Preaching' that 'Wit in the understanding is a sagacity to find out the nature, relations, and consequences of things'. The prose of King as exemplified in the last passage, however, leaves the rich, convoluted mode of an earlier civilization and strives to fulfill this dictum in the more formal, simple, and linear rhetoric of the Restoration.

Chapter 5

THE NOBLE ART

NINE years before the accession of Elizabeth (1549) was published a book, 'Very mete to be used of all sortes of people privately for their solace & comfort; laying apart all ungodly Songes and Ballades, which tende only to the norishment of vyce & corruption of youth. . . .' Thus Sternhold and Hopkins introduced their translation of the Psalms to England, beginning a long, often brilliant, yet still more often stultifying tradition of literary piety. Hundreds of editions were issued of this collection, and even after the savage tide of criticism which began at the end of the sixteenth century and eventually succeeded in putting it down, it left its impress on English psalmody by its meter and its diction. This collection owed its immediate success at least as much to the needs of the time as to its own limited merit; Protestantism speedily accepted this new, tangible form of worship as discovered, almost by Providence, to reward its intense spirit of devotion. In 1560 Bishop Jewel wrote:

Religion is now somewhat more established than it was. The people are everywhere exceedingly inclined to the better part. Ecclesiastical and popular music has very greatly helped it on. For, as soon as they had once commenced singing in public, in only one little church in London, immediately not only the neighbouring churches, but even far-distant cities, began to vie with each other in the same practice. You may sometimes see at Paul's Cross, after the sermon, six thousand persons, old men, boys, girls, singing and praising God together.[1]

Yet the state of psalmody, which satisfied piety, was

profoundly ¯unsatisfying to] the artist and critic. Among
the real and fancied intelligentsia opposition to the 'Old
Version' became increasingly rebellious. Some, like Bacon
or Sandys, themselves translated the Psalms of David.
Others, like Fuller, noted with considerable asperity that
the composers of the 'Old Version' had 'drank more of
Jordan than of Helicon', and that

> Later men have vented their just exceptions against the baldness
> of the translation; so that sometimes they make the Maker of the
> tongue to speak little better than barbarism, and have in many
> verses such poor rhyme that two hammers on a smith's anvil
> would make better music.[2]

Piety, however, was considerably in advance of poetry,
and, by the end of the seventeenth century, hundreds of
editions of the Psalms had appeared, by scores of authors,
all confirmed in a devout contempt for aesthetics.

Accompanying the shoal of editions of the Psalms was a
supporting yet contradictory body of theory. One tradition, very much on the defensive and hardly popular,
evolved from Wyatt, through Sidney to Sandys. This
tradition stood for utilization of secular poetical techniques
in psalmody. Its counterpart, the pietistic strain which
followed the 'Old Version', relied upon literal interpretation of the Psalms, conventional tunes, and monotonous
meter. To a generation fleeing the distractions of the
world an aesthetic commitment in psalmody was un-
important. It is evident that, in attempting to bring the
Psalms into the emotional and intellectual sphere of the
unlearned, Anglican psalmists, as well as Puritans, often
succeeded only in blunting their meaning, and arbitrarily
separating religion and art.

One of the most informative of sources for the pietistic
theory of translation is the Preface to William Barton's
The Book of Psalms in Metre. Close and Proper to the

Hebrew, . . . (1644). Barton produced this during the Commonwealth, at which time it enjoyed great approbation. The Preface is an explicit – as the translations themselves are an implicit – rejection of complexity in poetry. Barton bases his work on the conception that the function of a divine poem is principally the praise of God. His theory of translation reveals as no comment could the self-sought limitations of his work:

> If it be well consider'd how closely I have follow'd the Prose-Translation, I trust I shall never be blam'd for varying so much from the old Psalms. . . . . I have Compiled the whole Book (in all the first Metres especially) and in a great number of the second Metres as near as may be in the same order of words, and for the most part in as perfect Prose as Verse.[3]

Barton is explicit in his denial of being anything save an instrument of the word: 'I trust I shall never be blamed for any liberty used in my Translation'.[4] He provides a ready-made *apparatus criticus*, stating that whatever is in his translation is either

> 1 The very words of the Prose-Translation and (most what) in the same order, or 2 Words to the same effect, or 3 An allusion to a parallel Scripture, or 4 An amplification of the plain scope of the Text, or 5 An explication of the sense of it, or 6 and lastly, A truer or (at least) a fuller exposition of the Hebrew.[5]

While there would appear to be some loopholes for creativity, Barton took no chances on straying from the text.

The voluminous Preface to Simon Ford's *A New Version of the Psalms of David* (1688) is a source of information on the compromise of poetry with piety. Like Barton, Ford rejected secular poetic techniques; he in fact despised worldly poetry, believing that the only function of verse was the praise of the divine: 'Nor is it . . . less clear to any considering Persons, that the declination and debasement of that noble Art, to the service of those propensions of humane Nature which are more allyed to sensuality, is a meer perversion'.[6] In the rather morbidly pious tradition of Stubbs and Collier, Ford could state that secular poetry contains,

the foul and nasty Sinks and By-gutters, of lust and intemperance, flattery and malice; and every thing indeed, that tends to the immersing the humane soul the more deeply into all manner of viciousness and debauchery, by the means of that pleasure and delight, which Poetical measures commonly contribute to those Arguments about which they are imployed.[7]

Like Sidney, in the *Defence of Poetry*, Ford believes that holy poetry has morally cathartic qualities. It combines 'the delights of musick, with the precepts of Religion and Vertue',[8] and is therefore presumably a legitimate aesthetic form. Bearing in mind this Platonic concept, a kind of Christian-Doric strain of duty, we can understand more fully the temporizing he advocates between the highest poetry and the lowest understanding:

The design aimed at, by me in this version, was not to vaunt my skill in Poetry . . . nor was it, to entertain the devout inclinations of the more ingenious sort of Christians, with strains of elevated invention and expression, suited to their Genius. . . . But, that which I at first designed when I undertook this work, was meerly to render these pieces of holy writ, which are thought fit to be made parts of God's publick worship, in such a tolerable manner, as they might be for the use of all Christians; gratifying the more ingenious and learned Parts of all Congregations, with that smoothness and cleanness of style, which might make them not to nauseate it; and the more ordinary sort of those holy societies with that easiness and clearness of expression, which might not shoot over their heads. . . .[9]

Like King, Ford recognized two extremes which had prevailed in English psalmody. One mode was characterized by 'high flights of fancy, and . . . elaborate richness of language', the other by the literal terms which we have encountered in Barton. Like King also, Ford is convinced that his own performance avoids both 'heights of fancy' and 'flatness and dulness of invention, and expression'. We may say of his proud resolution to take a middle way, that the road to execrable poetry is paved with such intentions. The rest of his Preface carries on his aesthetic leveling. In the matter of rhyme, Ford states that he is willing to change any word at the request of his readers, which he can do 'with no great labour'. His concluding apology makes no bones of the fact that art and message are in no way related; he states that his work is not intended to 'represent to thee the true Genius and Spirit of that excellent vein of Poetry, with which the royal Psalmist wrote: But onely to transcribe the Piety and Devotion of his heavenly Poems, in words proper, and meet to beget like religious sentiments'.[10]

Not all translators felt obliged to surrender poetry for piety. Wither declared that the Psalms deserved the same attention as worldly poetry. In an eloquent passage Cowley argued for the same proposition:

All the *Books* of the *Bible* are either already most admirable, and exalted pieces of *Poesie*, or are the best *Materials* in the world for it. Yet, though they be in themselves so proper to be made use of for this purpose; None but a good *Artist* will know how to do it: neither must we think to cut and polish *Diamonds* with so little pains and skill as we do *Marble*. For if any man design to compose a *Sacred Poem*, by onely turning a story of the *Scripture*, like Mr *Quarles's*, or some other godly matter, like Mr *Heywood of Angels*, into *Rhyme*; He is so far from elevating of *Poesie*, that he onely abases *Divinity*. In brief, he who can write a *prophane Poem well*, may write a *Divine one better*; but he who can do that but ill, will do this much worse. The same fertility of *Invention*, the same wisdom of *Disposition*; the same *Judgement* in observance of *Decencies*, the same lustre and vigor of *Elocution*; the same modesty and majestie of *Number*; briefly the same kinde of *Habit*, is required to both.[11]

Sidney, Bacon, Phineas Fletcher, Habington, Milton, and Crashaw were part of the great tradition which believed in this doctrine. While these poets wrote little in the way of theory, their translations of the Psalms indicate full acceptance of the secular aesthetic. Sidney followed the faint trail of Wyatt, who in his version of the 'penitentiall' Psalms departed from literal tradition and traditional metrics. The metrical variety of Sidney was not his only contribution: we can see in Psalm *XIII* the brilliant personal note which was to be perfected in the poems of George Herbert:

> How long (ô Lord) shall I forgotten be?
> > What? ever?
> How long wilt thou thi hidden face from me
> > Dissever?
> How long shall I consult with carefull sprite
> > In anguish?
> How long shall I with foes triumphant might
> > Thus languish?
> Behold me Lord, let to thy hearing creep
> > My crying.
> Nay give me eyes, and light, least that I sleep
> > In dying.[12]

The poetic method of George Sandys was far advanced for his time; it is not only in his more powerful diction and conscious 'poetic' technique that he differs from most of his predecessors, but in the manner of conceiving the world of the Psalms. In his version of Psalm *LXV* he seems to delight in sensuous, pictorial nouns and adjectives, creating a kind of Rubens landscape. The original, a thanksgiving song, seems to be the barest sketch beside the richness of Sandys:

> He raine upon Earth's bosome powres;
> His swelling clouds abound with showres:

> And so prepares the lusty soile
> To recompense the Reapers' toile,
> Mellows the glebe with fatning juyce,
> Whose furrowes hopeful blades produce:
> With plenty crownes the smiling yeares,
> Shed from the influence of the spheares:
> The desert with sweet claver fills;
> And richly shades the joyful hils,
> Flocks cover all the higher plaine,
> The rancker valleyes cloth'd with graine.
> These in abundance solacing
> Without a tongue thy praises sing.[13]

Crashaw represented perhaps the *ne plus ultra* of artistic freedom. Some outstandingly individualistic (whatever else we are tempted to call them) lines of Psalm *XXIII* are these:

> Happy me! ô happy sheepe!
> Whom my God vouchsafes to keepe.
>
> At my feet the blubb'ring Mountaine
> Weeping, melts into a Fountaine,
> Whose soft silver-sweating streames
> Make high Noone forget his beames:
>
> How my head in ointment swims!
> How my cup orelooks her Brims![14]

Some few examples of the literal-minded school, on the other hand, should give us an idea of what King was up against. Here are Sternhold and Hopkins:

> And tho' ye were as black as pots,
> Your hue shall pass the dove
> Whose wings and feathers seem to have
> Silver and gold above.[15]

Here is the assiduous Henry Ainsworth, leader of the Amsterdam Separatists:

My soule with synners, gather not:
Nor with blood-guilty men my life.
In whose hands a mischeevous-plot:
whose right-hand is with bribes ful rife.[16]

Here is Baxter, who 'simply put the sentences of the Authorized Version into rhyme':[17]

Our age is threescore years and ten
    If (by strength) lengthened to fourscore
That strength our labour doth prolong
    And (doth but) make our sorrows more.[18]

Here is Henry Dod:

The Lord my gracious shepheard is
    So nothing want shall I.
In pastures greene he makes me rest
    by th-sweet streames leading me.[19]

And here, as a final exhibit, is Benjamin Keach, who wrote a great number of lines of religious poetry and several (necessary) apologies. His work perhaps culminated in *The Feast of Fat Things full of Marrow* (1696). The following hymn, which I take the liberty of reproducing in a chapter actually devoted to the more formal psalm, gives a sufficient taste of the triumph of piety over poetry:

SAINTS THE SALT OF THE EARTH

If saints, O Lord, do season all
    Amongst whom they do live,
Salt all with grace, both great and small,
    They may sweet relish give.

And, blessed be Thy glorious name!
    In England salt is found,
Some savoury souls who do proclaim
    Thy grace, which doth abound.

But O the want of Salt, O Lord!
  How few are salted well!
How few are like to salt indeed!
  Salt thou thy Israel!

Now Sing, ye saints who are this salt,
  And let all seasoned be
With your most holy gracious lives;
  Great need of it we see.

The earth will else corrupt and stink;
  O salt it well, therefore,
And live to Him that salted you,
  And sing for evermore.[20]

Henry King had strong opinions about psalmody, as he did about nearly anything else. His congratulatory poem to George Sandys, who had just published his volume of holy songs (1638), indicates that King had a rather sophisticated knowledge of the tradition. He pointed out that Sternhold and Hopkins' version, 'not diff'ring from a barbarous tongue', should be replaced on philological grounds, if for nothing else, since,

it was well, considering the time,
Which scarcely could distinguish verse and rhime.
But now the language, like the Church, hath won
More lustre since the Reformation.

He does not omit a slash or two at the literalists, who, like the exponents of the 'naked' manner in sermon rhetoric,

think God served best by their neglect.
Holding the cause would be profan'd by it,
Were they at charge of learning or of wit.

The implication is that the psalms, like every other cultural manifestation, have been denuded of beauty and meaning by the party dedicated to affected, enthusiastic plainness. Henry Dod is singled out as a particular example of zealous ineptitude. Dod's psalms, 'turn'd out of reason into rhime', were perhaps a legitimate butt for criticism, for he seems to have been the worst of the worst.

Even the translation of holy song then, could have overtones of the wider cultural conflict. King is almost too conscious, too aware of the split in his world. He sees the contamination of Puritanism not only in sermon rhetoric, but in the aesthetic of poetry. Committed to the rich and complex ideas of art of the Metaphysical school, he identifies the new 'rustick plainnesse' with the purposeful barbarity of the entire reforming movement. It must have seemed to him that the destruction of the cathedral at Chichester and the democratization of psalmody were, in some sense, different aspects of the same iconoclasm. There were unspoken rules even in poetry, and those who think 'God served best by their neglect' are attacking the world of art as they have already attacked the heavenly city of Jacobean order. His rebirth then, into the aesthetic of the later seventeenth century, was not an easy one. It did not require a critic of great perceptiveness to recognize in Sandys's translation one of the great performances of the century. Nor did it require much imagination to see that, in the protracted conflict, such a virtuoso performance was on the losing side.

When it was time for King to bring out his own translation, he felt compelled to take a less ideal, if equally censorious position. He realized that psalmody was part of the war of ideologies, and that it would be a signal victory for the orthodox party to win the hearts of men through holy song. But he could not in honesty adopt the rhetorical mores of a Rous or a Barton. He tried to define a 'Middleway' in translation, between literalism and poetic elegance

– and, of course, he failed. His optimistic letter to Archbishop Ussher, in which he is so obviously aware of the
traditional problems of translation, makes his failure rather
sad:

> I was (I confess) discouraged, knowing that Mr *George Sandys*,
> and lately one of our praetended Reformers,[21] had failed in Two
> different Extreams; The First too elegant for the vulgar use,
> changing both the Meter and Tunes wherewith they had been long
> acquainted; the Other as flat and poor, as lamely worded and un-
> handsomly rhimed as the Old; which, with much confidence, he
> undertook to amend. My Lord, I now come forth, an Adventurer
> in a Middle-way, whose aim was, without affectation of Words, to
> leave them not disfigured in the Sense.[22]

This new version, although provoked partially by
aesthetic indignation, was intended, like Ford's later
version, for the 'meanest understanding'. Bowing to the
time-sanctified grip of Sternhold and Hopkins on the
popular mind, King declared, 'I have therefore by tying
my self to the old Meter and Old Tunes, endeavoured to
prevent that disturbance which the Alteration might
bring'.[23] It is difficult to impeach King when he is so
forthright about classifying his own work. He recognizes
that it is a concession of artistry to popular taste, and of
intellect to habit:

> Wherein I shall desire my aime may be rightly understood, which
> was to render Them rather with perspicuity and plainesse for the
> vulgar use, then Elegance. For this the disadvantage of the Measure
> (of All others least gracefull) wherein most of the Psalmes run,
> allowes not: especially when by designe I deny my selfe the liberty
> of those words and Phrases, which either suit not the Gravity of the
> Subject, or capacity of the Meanest. To this end I have so closely
> followed the New Translation of the Psalms in our Church Bibles,
> that He who is able to read the one, may perceive the Reason of the
> Text nether lost, nor abused in the Rhime; Both which without

much Un evennesse, or force are brought to an easy and familiar agreement.[24]

Pietism alone was not responsible for his limitation, for it is clear that King shared none of the objections to secular poetry of many of his contemporaries. His theory of translation, like his theory of prose style, appears to be part of the growing movement in the seventeenth century toward literary simplicity, a movement which, in King, can be seen as both conscious and uncertain, if not painful. There seems to be little doubt that writers like Barton and Ford also expressed a part of the feeling of the age, and that their theories, limiting as they were, did aim at lucidity. The difference between the enlightened application of 'perspicuity' by Dryden and the stodgy, deadening application made by the pietists was the difference between art and morality.

King's 'Middle-way' involved a reasonable freedom for paraphrase. Conformity to the text of the scriptures was not the sole test of excellence, for the spirit of the Word, he believed, could sometimes best be manifested by circumlocution. Nor did it involve the customary tedious diction of the literal tradition of translation. The meter was the same, and the tunes the same, but poetry managed to creep into his new text: the Petrarchan sonnet, as well as the renditions of George Sandys, furnished some glowing adjectives and emotional, if hackneyed, phrases. While King was consciously reluctant to duplicate biblical metaphor – which he felt was an 'Elegance' impossible to re-create – he did, very occasionally, adapt Metaphysical images and ingenuity of reasoning. Ultimately, however, he is bound to a simplistic mode of rhyme, meter, and statement, which evades the necessary complexity of the songs of David. He is but a way-station on the road to Dryden.

Some of King's obvious failures resulted from his use of the common meter, which, with a rhyme scheme like the following (aa bb), could not have been worse for a system of lines of alternating length:

> The man is blest whose feet not tread,
> By wicked counsailes led.
>
> *   *   *   *   *
>
> Nor joynes himself unto the chaire,
> Where Scorners seated are.

John Patrick, while he noted that King had avoided the strict use of the 'words of the English Text, which in a Thousand places cannot be made to fall Naturally, without botching, into verse', noted also that he

> Yet pitched upon an unlucky method in his Translation, to make every first and second, every third and fourth line of a Psalm to answer and rhime to one another; whereby, in the short measures especially of eight and six feet, (which is the common one) he was too much hamper'd and confined, so that the words could not fall in so naturally as they ought.[25]

The awkwardness of Psalm *I*, above, is matched throughout his psalter. The stiffness of the 'Old Version's' meter needed only the recurring rhyme to point up its inadequacy. There are psalms of Sternhold and Hopkins which read more fluently than King's simply because the rhyme of every second line does not exaggerate the disparity of meter.

When King departs from this uncomfortable form, and writes, for example, in octosyllabic couplets (Psalm *XXII*), he tends to run head-on into another problem; in the pursuit of rhyme, he loses intelligence. He appears, at times, to share with Ford the conception that an answering chime is the summa of poetical form:

My God, My God, upon me look;
O wherefore hast Thou me forsook?
Why helps't Thou not, when I implore?
Nor hear'st, when I through anguish roare?[26]

As he would wish, the structure here is simple, the diction
monosyllabic or dissyllabic, and the meaning plain. Yet
such verse is travesty. It reminds us of nothing so much as
the psalms of the regrettable Henry Dod, which were
burnt by the hangman (I should like to believe) because
even that devout century had some poetical scruples.

Another rhyme scheme used by King in Psalm *L* is
distinguished by blundering inversion and a total absence
of harmony:

> That I require
>   Bulls flesh, why should'st thou think,
> Burnt in the fire?
>   Or blood of goats would drink?[27]

King may not have copied Rous, but the model was
available in 'Of bullocks eat the flesh, or drink the blood
of goats will I'.

Still another, in Psalm *XC*, leads to a primer-like flatness resembling Baxter's when it attempts to translate
purely literally:

> The common Age of mortall men
> Exceeds not Threescore years and ten.
> And if to Fourscore they attaine,
> Their life is but a length'ned paine.
> Incessant sorrowes, and disease,
> Their faculties, and vigour seize.
> For soon cut off our dayes decay,
> And suddenly we flie away.[28]

While King undeniably went beyond the 'Old Version'
in poetic diction, his own was not an unqualified success.
In his verse we find what are already the clichés of the

Petrarchan tradition, the 'grieved heart', 'sorrowes smart', 'heated breast', 'weeping eye', 'hopes forlorn', and the like. These terms do not seem really to suffice to bring out the stark meditative qualities of the original. When his version of Psalm *LXXXVIII* is compared to the Authorized Version, the artificiality of diction and emotionally dry couplet are seen to contain only the shell of the original. Adjective and substantive, cliché and empty pathos give only a truncated version of the fullness and profundity of the Psalm:

AUTHORIZED VERSION

Mine eye mourneth by reason of affliction:
Lord, I have called daily upon thee, I have
stretched out my hands unto thee.
Wilt thou shew wonders to the dead? Shall
the dead arise and praise thee? Selah.
Shall thy loving kindness be declared in the
grave? Or thy faithfulness in destruction?
Shall thy wonders be known in the dark? and
thy righteousness in the land of forgetfulness?

KING

My weeping eye doth daily mourne,
My hands stretch'd out, my hopes forlorne,
Wilt thou shew wonders to the dead,
To praise Thee rais'd and wakened?
Shall the devouring grave declare,
How true thy promis'd mercies are?
Or shall the dark Thy wonders see,
The Land were all forgotten be?

King was too good a poet to be perpetually confined by a delusive idea of simplicity. Some of his Psalms, like the following (Psalm *CVII*), reveal a unique ability to compress the matter of the original and to form a coherent stanza. A comparison with William Barton's version is helpful; in Barton, verbiage helps the meter to stumble along. His 'imployed for their gain' and 'upon the watery main', among others, seem to be designed more for the purpose of padding than for a richer picture or idea. It is worth noting that by a tacit return to conceit King acknowledges the need for a more than literal mode of apprehension. In this selection there are intimations of Augustan poetry; while both diction and syntax strive for the 'simplicity' of the closed couplet, the 'wit' of an earlier age attempts to construe an imaginative idea of elemental violence:

KING

They that in ships their trafick keep,
Behold Gods wonders in the deep.
For he commands the storme to blow,
Whose billowes them to heaven throw:
Then downe they fall, as if their graves
Were made beneath the gaping waves.
They stagger to and fro, and reele,
And like a drunkard rowls the keele.[29]

BARTON

They that descend to sea in ships,
imployed for their gain
In necessary merchandize
upon the watery main;
These men do God's rare works behold,
and no men more than these
Do see his wonders manifold
within the deepest seas.
For by the word of his command
he makes fierce winds to rise,
And lifteth up the rouling waves
unto the very skies.

> They mount to heaven, then they roul
> down to the deeps below;
> And by and by their very soul
> doth melt because of woe.
>
> They reel and stagger to and fro,
> like drunkards in their fits,
> And like unto distracted men
> Are put besides their wits.[30]

Again, to use Barton as a foil, we can see how King constructs a more intense image, and adapts the conceit to translation. While Barton talks unrestrainedly of 'darkness' and 'light', King's grave conceits re-create a perceptive, emotional experience:

KING

> If I pretend the darknes shall
> Upon me, like a cov'ring fall;
> Those heavy fogs, those mists of night,
> Will quickly cleare, and turne to light.
> The thickest shade, or blackest cloud,
> Can nothing from thy knowledg shrow'd:
> For darkness doth like Noon-tide shine,
> Light'ned by brighter beams of Thine.[31]

BARTON

> And if I say, the darkness sure
> shall hide me from thy sight:
> The darkness which is most obscure,
> about me shall be light.
> Yea, darkness hides not from thy sight:
> but night as day shines clear:
> To thee the darkness and the light
> do both alike appear.[32]

The same Psalm indicates a characteristically Metaphysical intelligence in King. He writes of the immanence of growth in 'substance', and conveys the idea of inchoate creation maturing into intelligibility. His couplet has an intellectual bias:

> Thou saw'st how my imperfect frame
> By daily growth to figure came.

It is unlike Barton's rather lame and incurious conclusion:

> Thine eye did see my substance rude,
> thy book nam'd every limb,
> Which by degrees were fashioned,
> when yet was none of them.

Ford's version, with the line, 'no joynt was lost, not one misplac'd', gives some idea of the varying approaches to literalness. Sometimes the translations were more of an enigma than the original.

Finally, it seems evident that King sometimes was able to re-create the spirit of his original. He used anthropomorphic imagery to an even greater extent than the Authorized Version in the following example, so that the unity of inanimate nature is even more richly described. Here are lines from Psalm *LXXVII*:

> The waters saw thee, O God, the waters saw
> thee; they were afraid: the depths also
> were troubled.
> The clouds poured out water: the skies sent
> out a sound: thine arrows also went abroad.

He tried to make of them the same kind of detailed imaginative picture so often attempted by Sandys:

> O God the waters at Thy sight
> Unto their depths retir'd with fright:
> The billowes of the troubled maine
> Shrunk downe, and hid themselves againe.

> The melting cloud discharg'd in showres,
> Like to a falling tempest powres:
> Whilst sounds of horrour teare the sky,
> And through the aire thine arrowes fly.[33]

King's Psalms, in short, generally abide by the literal theories of translation then admired. Like many translations based on the concept of prosaic literalness, they were short of aesthetic value. When King tacitly evaded the restrictions which he himself had praised, and adapted poetical techniques of the secular tradition, his Psalms reached a limited success. For the most part, however, a terribly confining rhyme scheme and a destructive obsession with simplicity of language and idea spoiled his efforts in the field. He is one of the rare examples of a competent poet who consciously laid aside his competence.

Chapter 6

POETRY AND THE TRADITION

IN the terms of Robert Penn Warren, Metaphysical poetry is, fortunately, among the least 'pure' of poetical forms.[1] It insists that we do not 'purge out all complexities'. Even among the Metaphysicals, however, there was 'pure' and 'impure' poetry. In the occasional poetry of the Metaphysicals evidence may be found for a conflict between creativeness, which disrupts the 'purity' of a poem, and formula, which strives to fulfill that 'purity'. In the poetry of Henry King, whose Metaphysical inheritance was diluted by a simpler logic than that of his great example, Donne, we are forced to recognize something about occasional poetry. In his finest examples King's insistence is on complicating and transcending a formula. Most verse performances of the occasional type adhere to formulas of praise, grief, or some other form of commemoration. Even when they employ devices of trope or paradox they are rarely complex or subtle, or capable of juxtaposing elements not immediately relevant to the superficial statement. They rarely give a more profound identity to a poem than that conferred by mere social observance.

The best poetry of occasion, while capable of the utmost simplicity, can expand suddenly and escape its overt occasion to a more inclusive theme. The poet and his statement become assimilated into a poem, the celebration of the specific occasion is only the reason. An analogy might be drawn between this and the mythical inscription for the ponderous Gothic façade of Yale's

Sterling Library, 'this is not the library, the library is inside'.

In the poetry of King sometimes the precise reverse is true. There are occasional poems which, in spite of refinements in technique, remain superficial. While we admit the necessity of poetry which does not 'assault the Absolute', we feel instinctively that to abandon some necessary involvement of the mind and emotions is to invite banality. The total effect, intellectually, becomes that of a greeting card. Such poetry has always been largely social. It is communicated to an individual or to a specified audience, rather than to the world. By standards of the seventeenth century such poetry could indicate such widely disparate things as an ideological sympathy or a gracious gesture. It could identify a recipient, establish an idea, or commemorate an event. But the best poetry of this kind, like Jonson on Penshurst, Milton on Edward King, or Marvell on Nun-Appleton House, attempts to add something to a recognized convention. The poem is an act of civilization; it stresses the community of regard among the literate. The object is spiritually interesting, or at least strikes sparks from the poet. The poet can, as Donne did, insist on the 'idea of woman', and symbolize in the guise of commemorating. He can say the many serious things which must be said between man and woman. In some forms, like the mystifying, *apparently* undisciplined elegies of the Metaphysical poets, he can use the immediate occasion as a pretext to enter into the mind, to be followed by a series of contingent opinions. In any case he takes the immediate occasion as statement to be amplified – or even negated – by the poem.

The complexities of Donne, who made something 'rich and strange' out of every outwardly innocent form, are often lacking in King. In, for example, 'Upon a Table-

Book presented to a Lady', or 'To the same Lady upon Mr: Burtons Melancholy', we find little beyond the poetic greeting card:

> If in this Glass of Humours you do find
> The Passions or diseases of your mind,
> Here without pain, you safely may endure,
> Though not to suffer, yet to read your cure.[2]

With his typical semi-conceit, a pattern of language which casts the occasion in mildly 'witty' rather than literal terms, he neatly dusts off the occasion. Communication has been established, a sentiment has been expressed, and (what Coleridge would identify as) fancy has been added. But I think we should agree that it is a highly limited poem.

There is a radical change in 'Upon a Braid of Hair in a Heart sent by Mrs E. H.' The entire poem is only six lines in length:

> In this small Character is sent
> My Loves eternal Monument.
> Whil'st we shall live, know, this chain'd Heart
> Is our affections counter-part.
> And if we never meet, think I
> Bequeath'd it as my Legacy.

The second line is perhaps purposeful in its trite magniloquence. It marks the conventional introduction, the conventional acknowledgment, the entire complex of courtly hyperbole. But something happens in each couplet which radically changes the poem. The tone of the second couplet drops to reflective precision. Its rhetoric does not bow down to the waist. Looking for a hyperbolical balance to the second line we are thrust off our psychological balance by finding only quiet assertion, and a far more abstract symbol. The third couplet is the most radical of all, for the locket has become something powerfully different from its first two incarnations. It is, in a sense, no longer the subject of the poem. The simple structure of the couplet is deceptive; the more it is read, the clearer one can see that the dissolution of life's tangencies, of life itself, is really the poem's end. 'And if we never meet' – surely we expect some line on the evocative powers of the memento, but we are confronted only by the impersonal, abstract, 'think I / Bequeath'd it as my Legacy'. The hyperbolical 'Monument' has become the final, flat 'Legacy', with all of its associations. The utter conventionality of the first symbolization is thoroughly nullified by the last. Yet this is not an 'assault' upon the Absolute, for it exists as a logical extension of the object, and of the occasion. The intellectual possibilities, to say nothing of the shifting emotional possibilities of the symbol, have been filled in. The measure of the poem is in its ability to transform a social gesture.

If our expectations are correct 'By occasion of the Young Prince his happy birth' will be one of the numberless, turgid poems to the royal infant, complete with muses, wise men, blessings of fortune, and all the other lares and penates of the laureate tribe. We might expect, for example, the panegyric of William Cartwright's 'On the Birth of the Duke of York, 1633'. The very least thing to expect is a strong exposition of an ironical poetical persona (the poet) and a witty equivalence between the birth of the prince and the death of the king. Instead of Cibberian assiduity, poetry which will 'sweetly flow thro' all the Royal Line', we are given a strong form of poetical egotism:

> At this glad Triumph, when most Poets use
> Their quill, I did not bridle up my Muse
> For sloth or less devotion. I am one

That can well keep my Holy-dayes at home;
That can the blessings of my King and State
Better in pray'r then poems gratulate;
And in their fortunes bear a loyal part,
Though I no bone-fires light but in my heart.

There is always the possibility of this being insincere in its sincerity; the following seems, however, to continue the pull away from conventional attitudes of encomium:

For howere Children, unto those that look
Their Pedigree in God's, not the Church book,
Fair pledges are of that eternitie
Which Christians possess not till they die;
Yet they appear view'd in that perspective
Through which we look on men long since alive,
Like succours in a Camp, sent to make good
Their place that last upon the watches stood.
So that in age, or fate, each following birth
Doth set the Parent so much neerer earth:
And by this Grammar we our heirs may call
The smiling Preface to our funerall.

This is in some way negating the overt convention which it pretends to serve. True to Donne's flamboyant logic, King allows his poetry to reveal what may follow – but ordinarily would not – from a given context. 'Decay is natures Kalendar' is a stock Metaphysical idea, but not a trite one in this context. The continuation of the poem is focused on the conceit that Charles I rules through Charles II, so is effectively 'alive', but to reason in genealogies is to evade the cold perception that the king will die and be replaced by his son. The theme, 'nor can / It hurt the King to think he is a man', has perhaps the dominant affective position. The poem is a vehicle by which the private discipline of the 'uncorrupted poet', whose character is more or less ironically sketched in the first lines of the poem, may force the royal occasion into a mold for his own honest and sardonic logic. Like Donne, he teases the subject along with paradox:

> if fathers should remain
> For ever here, children were born in vain;
> And we in vain were Christians, should we
> In this world dream of perpetuitie.

Like Juvenal, he takes the sardonic position 'mentiri nescio', a position taken by Marston, Hall, Swift, and Pope, all poets using the mask of the irascible, honest satirist.

Another poem, 'An Acknowledgment', does not, I think, need to be stretched very far to qualify as an occasional poem. As the poem develops, from a conventional opening in which the poet confesses his wish to remain forever bound to the lady addressed, to the extended conceit in which he identifies the occasion of the poem (he has been given a locket), we seem to be heading down a familiar path. He states:

> 'twas my fate your prisoner to be,
> Heav'n knows I nothing fear but libertie.

And,

> I might reckon ore
> Your vertues and my debt, which does surmount
> The trivial laws of Popular account.

He then reaches the point of the courtly conceit proper, or flattery astronomical:

> The sparkling constellation which combines
> The Lock, is your dear self, whose worth outshines
> Most of your sex: so solid and so clear
> You like a perfect Diamond appear;
> Casting from your example fuller light

> Then those dimme sparks which glaze the brow of night,
> And gladding all your friends, as doth the ray
> Of that East-starre which wakes the cheerful day.

As the conceit is enlarged to its final form we encounter a typically Metaphysical resistance. The poem's tenor is suddenly and violently shifted:

> But the black Map of death and discontent
> Behind that Adamantine firmament,
> That luckless figure which like Calvary
> Stands strew'd and coppy'd out in skuls, is I:
> Whose life your absence clouds, and makes my time
> Move blindfold in the dark ecliptick line.

Mr Williamson, in *The Donne Tradition*, calls this an example of Donnian 'awful fire', but it should have been examined as more than a strictly metaphorical moment. From here on the poem again flows smoothly to a courtly hopeless ending. Up to this point we have had the poetry of praise. This is the one point in the poem where the author permits himself to carry to a remarkably full expression the otherwise formalized hopelessness and darkness of the love convention. Placing it in a setting larger than life, emphasizing the spiritual blindness of his 'dark ecliptick line', he constructs a surrealistic, loosely bound series of images which effectively mix 'death and discontent'. The brilliance of the argument is in removing it from the personal; within the dark universe of the six lines there is no human figure posturing, but only the consciousness existing, blinded and suffering, in space. It is worth comparing this, the deeper perception of suffering, with the more truly conventional picture of the conclusion:

> Though my tempestuous fancie like the skie
> Travail with stormes, and through my watry eie
> Sorrows high-going waves spring many a leak;
> Though sighs blow loud til my hearts cordage break. . . .

For each successful juxtaposition of convention and Metaphysical wit in King, there are entire poems which are best passed over, like 'Upon the Kings happy return from Scotland', or 'To the Queen at Oxford'. They allow the formulas of encomium and sententiousness complete precedence. It would, therefore, not be accurate to claim that King, like Donne, completely revised the occasional poem to be an incisive instrument within his own discipline. The mass of King's addresses, while well-turned, make no challenge of great intellectual or emotional magnitude. They go about their stated business, but they do not much transcend the formula into which they are cast. Some poems even demonstrate that King could surrender to the facile traditions he himself attacked in 'To his unconstant Friend':

> I will not fall upon my pointed quill,
> Bleed ink and Poems, or invention spill
> To contrive Ballads, or weave Elegies
> For Nurses, wearying when the infant cries.

They are founded on familiar literary conventions rather than on the fiercely individual wit which illuminates something apart from the immediate, superficial context.

'O killing Rhetorick of Death'

When T. S. Eliot, in his criticism of the Metaphysical poets, praised their sensibility to death, he described the finest and smallest segment of Metaphysical poetry. The omnipresent topic of death was by no means so effectively used by Donne's followers as by Donne himself. One doubts whether they were totally conscious of the intensely personal recognition of death that Donne manifests, for in much of later seventeenth-century poetry death is simply a point of origin for verse. This need not be impugned necessarily, for any excuse for verse is legitimate; the danger for poetry is to use any inspiration with that habitual familiarity which fails to understand the inspiration, and which eventually turns it into a cliché. I am not referring to the necessity for the poet to demonstrate 'sincere' feeling; this is unlikely, and even undesirable.

The funeral elegy is a peculiarly good example of the social ritual embodied in occasional poetry. As a form it embodies a fundamental human necessity to acknowledge certain facts. At its very best, poetic insight into death, like Claudio's in *Measure for Measure*, registers a painfully clear imaginative vision. Or, like Donne's 'Relique', it uses symbolism to focus momentarily on man's fate. Another human attitude toward death, the ironic, is depicted in Marvell's 'To his Coy Mistress'. Such poetry acknowledges death as experience:

> Donne, I suppose, was such another
> Who found no substitute for sense,
> To seize and clutch and penetrate;
> Expert beyond experience.[3]

It is given to only a few, however, to perceive fully the core of meaning in a tradition. Death was generally personified, allegorized, wept over, scorned, castigated, and used as an excuse for heroic grief and exaggerated praise. For the most part, the funeral elegy, half-religious and more than half conventional, was a well-grooved rut of rhetoric.

Like most ritual, the funeral elegy had its standardized components. King's 'An Elegy Upon Prince Henry's death' exemplifies the super-emotional and cosmic styles of grief:

> Keep station Nature, and rest Heaven sure
> On thy supporters shoulders, lest past cure
> Thou dasht in ruine fall, by a griefs weight

Will make thy basis shrink, and lay thy height
Low as the Center. Heark! and feel it read
Through the astonisht Kingdom, Henry's dead.
It is enough; who seeks to aggravate
One strain beyond this, prove more sharp his fate
Than sad our doom. The world dares not survive
To parallel this woes superlative.
O killing Rhetorick of Death! two words
Breathe stronger terrours then Plague, Fire or Swords
Ere conquer'd. This were Epitaph and Verse
Worthy to be prefixt in Natures herse,
At Earths last dissolution; whose fall
Will be less grievous though more generall:
For all the woe ruine ere buried,
Throngs in this narrow compasse, Henry's dead.
Cease then unable Poetry, thy phrase
Is weak and dull to strike us with amaze
Worthy thy vaster subject.

In Donne's elegy on Prince Henry the same cosmic
heightening is employed. A modern critic has noted of
Donne's poem: 'We are today put off by the gross exaggeration of its adulation. Its ideas on reason and faith
represent Donne's maturest spirit, but they are applied to
Prince Henry's death in a manner at once overingenious
and cursory'.[4] She notes that its essential result is a
certain 'triviality'. King's poem also attempts to achieve
an inflated emotional state *in medias res*. The subject is
elevated to cosmic rank, and grief inflated proportion-
ately. It seems unlikely that 'the wit is finest and most
Donnian' in the image, 'O killing Rhetorick of Death' and
its development; at best there is only a certain verbal
cleverness. Donne's equipoise of meditation and feeling in
his *Anniversaries* is far more subtle, and involves a far
richer intellectual content. He tactfully allows his osten-
sible subject to disappear, and, when he writes of universal
dissolution, he gives chapter and verse citations.

In like manner the beginning of King's 'An Elegy Upon the most victorious King of Sweden Gustavus Adolphus' attempts, by the hyperbole of the 'killing Rhetorick of Death', to make a shrine of verse. The rush of undisciplined images, unconnected with any need except that of pounding out a *large* picture of grief, makes for quite a rococo shrine:

> Like a cold fatal sweat which ushers death
> My thoughts hang on me, & my lab'ring breath
> Stopt up with sighs: my fancie big with woes,
> Feels two twinn'd mountains struggle in her throws,
> Of boundless sorrow one, t'other of sin;
> For less let no one rate it to begin
> Where honour ends.

The poem, rather longer than most of his other elegies, exhibits some typical aspects of the funeral elegy. The first, of course, is dependence on a rhetoric of grief and portentousness. It is like Thomas Randolph's 'Upon the report of the King of Swedens Death':

> Can he be dead, and no portents appeare?
> No pale Ecclipse of th' sun to let us feare
> What we should suffer, and before his light
> Put out, the world inveloped in Night?

King's poem, too, exemplifies the widespread poetic magniloquence stimulated by Gustavus' demise. In varying degrees of intricacy such poetry also expands on the theme of incredulity and universal mourning, eulogy, admonition of Death, and, finally, comforting apotheosis. Carew's opinion of the futility of heroic elegy on this occasion was not widely shared:

> what though the German Drum
> Bellow for freedome and revenge, the noyse
> Concernes not us, nor should divert our joyes.[5]

Some of King's worst poetic platitudes are in his meditations dedicated to the proposition that flesh is grass. The nineteenth century took a melancholy pleasure in contemplating *sententiae* on the short life and sure death of man, if we judge by the popularity of 'Sic Vita' and 'The Dirge', both fairly representative of King's recurrent statements on 'this child of dust', this 'walking clay', etc.[6] Most of these meditations on life and eternity are stylized to the point of shallow fluidity:

> Life is a crooked Labyrinth, and we
>   Are daily lost in that Obliquity.
> 'Tis a perplexed circle, in whose round
> Nothing but sorrows and new sins abound.[7]

> Ill busi'd man! why should'st thou take such care
>   To lengthen out thy lifes short Kalendar?
> When e'ry spectacle thou lookst upon
> Presents and acts thy execution.[8]

These meditations were, in all probability, related to the great stream of thought – and fashion – analyzed by Louis Martz in *The Poetry of Meditation*. King, like Donne, took to heart the precept of the tradition of *Ars Moriendi*, that

The house of earth (which is our grave) is the schoole of true wisdom, where almighty God is wont to teach those that be his. There he teacheth them how great is the vanity of this world . . . there he teacheth them to know themselves, which is one of the most highest points of Philosophy which may be learned.[9]

King's declaration in his funeral sermon on Brian Duppa, 'The Grave is commonly as powerful an Oratour as the Pulpit, and by presenting the fears of an Ill Death instructs us in the Rules of a Good Life',[10] indicates that he was conscious of the unique morality of the funereal. His meditations have almost nothing, however, of what Professor Martz calls 'the full self-awareness' of the vision of Donne or Herbert.

If he became preoccupied with the pretentious and the banal he also rose above this. In writing specifically literary tributes in the form of elegy, King was far from conventional. One of his finest elegies is 'Upon the death of my ever desired friend Doctor Donne Dean of Pauls'. This poem is charged with rhetorical vitality. Like his elegy on Ben Jonson, it seems to leave the genre of funeral poetry and take its place in the great tradition of the critical poem. It is an address by one mind to another, strictly in the light of certain intellectual and spiritual obligations. The poem is, in fact, not so much about Donne as it is about his relationship to the mystique of poetry. King begins with the paradoxical tone which is to recur in the verse:

> To have liv'd eminent in a degree
> Beyond our lofty'st flights, that is like thee;
> Or t'have had too much merit is not safe;
> For such excesses find no Epitaph.

With his almost predictable partiality for contrast, he strokes in the world of time and place, which is to be continually contrasted with the supernatural brilliance of the dead poet:

> At common graves we have Poetick eyes
> Can melt themselves in easie Elegies;
> Each quill can drop his tributary verse,
> And pin it, like the Hatchments, to the Herse.

'Common graves', 'Poetick eyes', 'tributary verse', need no further explanation to define their earthbound nature. The contrast to their frigidity is expressed in the growing excitement of his devout, hyperbolical rhetoric on the spirit of Donne:

> But at thine, Poem or inscription
> (Rich Soul of wit and language:) we have none;
> Indeed a silence does that Tomb befit
> Where is no Herald left to blazon it.
> Widdow'd invention justly doth forbear
> To come abroad, knowing thou art not here,
> Late her great Patron; whose prerogative
> Maintain'd and cloth'd her so, as none alive
> Must now presume to keep her at thy rate,
> Though he the Indies for her dowre estate:
> Or else that awful fire, which once did burn
> In thy clear brain, now fall'n into thy Urn,
> Lives there, to fright rude Empericks from thence,
> Which might profane thee by their Ignorance.
> Who ever writes of thee, and in a style
> Unworthy such a Theme, does but revile
> Thy precious dust, and wake a learned spirit
> Which may revenge his rapes upon thy merit.
> For all a low-pitcht fancie can devise,
> Will prove at best but hallow'd injuries.

The opposition between Donne and those who 'melt themselves in easie Elegies', is not developed in the dialectical style of Carew, whose elegy on Donne runs through a concrete series of statements on the poet's accomplishment. It is the purpose of this poem to express something else about Donne. King, it seems to me, writes of Donne as if he *is* what he symbolizes. The images describing him are strangely ethereal, 'Rich Soul of wit', 'awful fire', 'learned spirit', as if he does not represent the high artistic purpose of poetry so much as he embodies it. There is an impersonal quality in his description: if Carew sees Donne as a Promethean among poets, King sees him as a part of the spirit of poetry, a combination of the prophetic vates and the punishing Nemesis. What he is saying is that there is no true knowledge of Donne. He *is*, his accomplishments need no catalogue.

Like Milton writing on Shakespeare, King seems to mistrust his own powers of comprehension. The penultimate stanza gives both the highest praise and no praise at all in its conceits. The desolation of poetry, the paradox of attempting to write on the indescribable, are evident:

> Commit we then Thee to Thy self: nor blame
> Our drooping loves, which thus to thine own fame
> Leave Thee Executour: since but thine own
> No pen could do Thee Justice, nor Bayes crown
> Thy vast desert; save that, we nothing can
> Depute to be thy ashes Guardian.

The ultimate epigram on which the poem rests is a restrained summation of its purpose. We must turn, King says, to the poetry of the master-spirit himself to perceive his power:

> So Jewellers no Art or Metal trust
> To form the Diamond, but the Diamonds dust.

And the very character of the lines helps us also to perceive Donne's influence. King, in these last lines, with the self-effacing honesty of the disciple, yet with the rhetorical method of the master, is indicating that his own inability to describe Donne is, after all, in the tradition of Donne himself. If he is the 'Diamonds dust', we can see that his solemn conceits on the dead poet are derived from that poet, that the intellectual decorum of King's poetry exists only because the great exemplar showed the way. The poem is a balance of contrasts. Donne is contrasted to the army of poetasters, the 'rude Empiricks' of the world. King contrasts his subject with his evident inability to describe it. Finally, with a really Donnian twist, King subtly contrasts his own 'persona' of intelligent honesty working through the conceit, with the evident inspiration, who is also its subject. On the one hand he completely effaces himself from the scene of poetry, on the other, he asserts that, in the act of negation, he is perceiving poetry in the manner of Donne. He is, after all, if we follow the logic, making something (the poem) out of nothing (his refusal to create a poem).

The terse and precise lines on Sir Walter Ralegh represent also the willing abandonment of the 'killing Rhetorick of Death':

> I dare not then so blast thy memory
> As say I do lament or pity thee.
> Were I to choose a subject to bestow
> My pity on, he should be one as low
> In spirit as desert – That durst not dy
> But rather were content by slavery
> To purchase life: or I would pity those
> Thy most industrious and friendly foes:
> Who when they thought to make thee scandals story
> Lent thee a swifter flight to Heav'n and glory.
> That thought by cutting off some wither'd dayes,
> (Which thou could'st spare them) to eclipse thy praise;
> Yet gave it brighter foil, made thy ag'd fame
> Appear more white and fair, then foul their shame:
> And did promote an Execution
> Which (but for them) Nature and Age had done.

King avows that he will not 'lament or pity'; like his poem on Donne, this is an exercise of rational contrasts. There is a contrast between the sublime Ralegh, who requires no pity, and the man 'as low / In spirit as desert', who needs the artificial strength of eulogy. There is the contrast between the court clique, who succeeded in ruining Ralegh, and his fame, which they succeeded only in increasing. There is a contrast too, although less overt,

between the language of this poem and that of the tradition. This is couched in hard, Jonsonian terms. The words
are short, pungent, seemingly designed to place as much
emphasis as possible on the extemporaneous character of
their delivery. The description progresses from the unadorned lines of the beginning to a curtailed metaphorical
style, in which the 'wither'd dayes', 'brighter foil', and
'ag'd fame' are the more effective for their apparently
dispassionate and final characterization. The deceptive
simplicity of the rhetoric seems to endow the speaker with
sincerity, and the subject with rectitude.

Even in his elegy on Gustavus Adolphus, whose beginning is certainly dedicated to the 'Keep station Nature . . .'
school of lament, he can occasionally escape the turgid
metaphor and ponderous imagery of the funereal tradition.
He adapts the compass image of Donne for a difference
purpose, which has its own form of substantiating logic:

> Yet since it was decreed thy lifes bright Sun
> Must be eclips'd ere thy full course was run,
> Be proud thou didst in thy black Obsequies
> With greater glory set then others rise.
> For in thy death, as life, thou heldest one
> Most just and regular proportion.
> Look how the Circles drawn by Compass meet
> Indivisibly joyned head to feet,
> And by continued points which them unite
> Grow at once Circular and Infinite:
> So did thy Fate and Honour now contend
> To match thy brave beginning with thy end.
> Therefore thou hadst instead of Passing bells
> The Drums and Cannons thunder for thy knells;
> And in the Field thou did'st triumphing dy,
> Closing thy eye-lids with a victory:
> That so by thousands who there lost their breath
> *King-like* thou might'st be waited on in death.

King relies on the ancient idea of the perfection of form, and the circle is the most perfect, most 'powerful' of all forms, the symbol of complete proportion and infinite progression. When he makes his initial statement on the life and death of the hero his purpose is not only to declaim on greatness, but to symbolize the constancy and irresistible arc-like progress of Gustavus' career. The military precision of 'Most just and regular proportion', endows his career with something of the mathematical finality of the circle. There is the implication that Gustavus, far above the power of man, forced this pattern of 'just and regular proportion' upon life, as the compass imposes the 'Circular and Infinite' form on a plane.

This imposition of idea upon life is painted in the all-embracing scene of the last six lines. Death itself becomes transposed for the hero; instead of the forced equality of life's last scene Gustavus caps his 'brave beginning' with his glorious end. As if he were writing, to paraphrase Donne, not about the king, but about the idea of the king, the poet envisions the superhuman affirmation of a royal will. The act of death is part of a great symbolic rite, in which the significance of the 'Circular and Infinite' life is recapitulated.

King's most famous poem is on death, yet it is clearly not an ordinary funeral elegy, nor an expanded epitaph like his literary elegies. 'The Exequy' stands with poetry like 'In Memoriam' as part of a small group of effective personal poems of grief and meditation. No conception of the fullness of Metaphysical poetry on death would be complete without awareness of this poem. One can approach it only with a certain degree of trepidation.

Unlike the four other great elegies of our language, by Milton, Gray, Shelley, and Tennyson, this poem contains no elements of the pastoral, no sublimated wish for fame, no querying of the universal plan. Unlike most of the elegies of its particular milieu, it is not about a great figure who is mourned publicly by all, and privately by none. Even among the works of its author it is *sui generis*, a love poem on death. It is not a modern poem, nor easily understood by moderns. 'The Exequy' antedates 'Lycidas' by rather more than half of a significant generation. Written in the world of order of King James, it differs in temper from the other elegies of our experience. John Crowe Ransom has stated that 'Lycidas' has the tone – the skepticism, the hard individualism – of modernity. 'The Exequy' has another temper entirely, for it is not concerned with the world as we know it. The other great elegies are conscious attacks on their world. They try to form some kind of tenable synthesis on the meaning of living. This is a retreat to another world, the isolated microcosm of the two lovers so often imagined in the work of John Donne.

If there was anything that Henry King might have learned from Donne it was the artistry of love. He learned sometime in 1624 to see with painful intensity that the woman of flesh and the woman of symbol could be one. He wrote in 'The Exequy', as Donne had in the *Anniversaries*, of a metaphysical experience which could alone embody the sense of 'the heart being perish'd'. He learned from Jonson, himself a master of the restrained elegy, that it was possible to write of this experience in simple, masculine, and direct terms. And he was able to draw on the great Jacobean sermons, on the poetic metaphors which sprang from the common European Latin tradition, and on the language of the new science. All this he learned, and how to subdue it to his senses. When, about 1630, he wrote his second poem about Anne Berkeley

King, 'The Anniverse', he could say with prosaic accuracy of the past six years:

> thou wilt bind me living to a coarse,
> And I must slowly waste. . . .

It was an accurate description as well of his earlier poem, which mingled love and death in a manner 'expert beyond experience'.

We are made aware in the first couplet that an expression beyond conventional grief is in the making:

> Accept thou Shrine of my dead Saint,
> Insteed of Dirges this complaint.

Almost immediately King enters the realm of Donne, the witty poetry of deadly seriousness, where conceit sharpens the intensity of feeling:

> Dear loss! since thy untimely fate
> My task hath been to meditate
> On thee, on thee: thou art the book,
> The library whereon I look
> Though almost blind. For thee (lov'd clay)
> I languish out, not live the day,
> Using no other exercise
> But what I practise with mine eyes:
> By which wet glasses I find out
> How lazily time creeps about
> To one that mourns: this, onely this
> My exercise and bus'ness is:
> So I compute the weary houres
> With sighs dissolved into showres.

The logic of the conceits reveals a certain state of mind, which finds fit expression only in the elaboration of paradox. The tone and language of paradox underlay this poem, for it is in a certain sense the ultimate form of reasoning. To reason by paradox is to be aware of the impotence of reason itself. The verse begins with a medi-

tation, but it is not, as the reader would expect, a holy meditation on the living God. The religious 'exercise' of which
he speaks is concentrated on earthly love – and on 'earth'.
He describes his own consciousness, but it is a consciousness paralyzed. Blindness is profoundly symbolic. The act
of will, the strength itself of meditation, is numbed by the
senses. Blinded spiritually, bound 'living to a coarse', the
poet is cut off from the world of reality, and immured in
another world. He is within the 'Adamantine firmament'
described so briefly in 'An Acknowledgment'. The tragic
predicament of the mind is its existence in a world where
time and grief are equivalent. The various conceits of the
passage are recapitulations of this idea. The elements of
time serve only to delineate the pervasive qualities of grief.
Although the poet is aware that he exists in time, he exists
in grief as well. The last conceit indicates that the two
things can be almost literally fused.

As yet the conceits are fragmentary. The conceits of the
book, of tears, and of sighs come from the great storehouse
of Latin elegiac verse. The mind is benumbed, and seeks
in the conventional an answer to its deprivation. But the
world of grief intimated must become explicit, described
in a powerful elaborated conceit of universal proportions.
The 'little world' of the lovers so familiar in the 'Songs and
Sonets' is now become a larger world, one far more real to
the consciousness than the one which merely afflicts our
senses. It is the world described by the cosmic science of
infinity. Time and being, the two subjects of the imagery
of the opening, are developed and transformed:

> Nor wonder if my time go thus
> Backward and most preposterous;
> Thou hast benighted me, thy set
> This Eve of blackness did beget,
> Who was't my day, (though overcast

Before thou had'st thy Noon-tide past)
And I remember must in tears,
Thou scarce had'st seen so many years
As Day tells houres. By thy cleer Sun
My life and fortune first did run;
But thou wilt never more appear
Folded within my Hemisphear,
Since both thy light and motion
Like a fled Star is fall'n and gon,
And twixt me and my soules dear wish
An earth now interposed is,
Which such a strange eclipse doth make
As ne're was read in Almanake.

The collapse of the order of the universe is figured through metaphors of time. In its most essential and visible form, its God-ordained cleavage into night and day, it has been corrupted. It would not be far wrong to think of 'Darkness at Noon' as symbolically relevant, for the 'Eve of blackness' is an unnatural 'strange eclipse' of unfulfilled innocence. The 'cleer Sun' with its 'light' and 'motion' has been eclipsed by the purposely ambiguous 'earth'. There is no harmony, no meaning in the universe.

It is still the tone of paradox, that ultimate form of reasoning, which, more intensely than any other mode, confronts what is and what should be. And now the language of ambiguity becomes more insistent. 'Blackness', like blindness, is spiritual. 'Beget', the giving of life, has fathered death. The 'Hemisphear' of the macrocosm and the circle of the lover's arms have been broken at once. 'Earth' has come between the planets – as earth has covered the face of the loved one in her grave.

The poem is in many ways a paradigm of the operation of the mind. It changes its tenor now, although the fundamental idea of time still dominates the consciousness.

The poet momentarily retreats to the mythological vision
which began the elegaic tradition:

> I could allow thee for a time
> To darken me and my sad Clime,
> Were it a month, a year, or ten,
> I would thy exile live till then;
> And all that space my mirth adjourn,
> So thou wouldst promise to return;
> And putting off thy ashy shrowd
> At length disperse this sorrows cloud.

But the clouded vision of an Orpheus and his Eurydice is
confronted by a dark and permanent truth. Christianity
itself furnishes the final transformation of the lovers and
of time. At first it is that bitterly awaited time between us
and our judgment. Finally time will be eternity. Death has
been grief, it must now be hope:

> But woe is me! the longest date
> Too narrow is to calculate
> These empty hopes: never shall I
> Be so much blest as to descry
> A glimpse of thee, till that day come
> Which shall the earth to cinders doome,
> And a fierce Feaver must calcine
> The body of this world like thine,
> (My Little World!). That fit of fire
> Once off, our bodies shall aspire
> To our soules bliss: then we shall rise,
> And view our selves with cleerer eyes
> In that calm Region, where no night
> Can hide us from each others sight.

This is the language and the apocalyptic vision of the
Jacobean sermon. There is in it a certain destructive
honesty. It mingles despair over mortality with the profoundly Christian vision of the world to come; this act of

reasoning itself being one of the great themes of seventeenth-century Christianity. But the poem outgoes what I should describe as this cultural habit. It deals with the conventional idea of apotheosis in a more somber and naked manner than 'Lycidas'. While the 'little world' of the lovers will be burned, purified, and resurrected – 'sunk low', at first,

> but mounted high,
> Through the dear might of him that walk'd the waves

it is almost impossible to find in the verse of apotheosis an equally sharp awareness of the destruction of the body. Nor is it very often that we will find the complex yet unified awareness of the two worlds ('The body of this world like thine') which must be destroyed to attain the final vision of being. The two lovers, apart in their 'world', are yet part of the terrifying, immutable cosmic process. The play on 'world' has a typically manifold Metaphysical focus, on the 'Little World' of her body, on the world of the lovers, and finally on the world which is beyond their will to affect, which imprisons them in time and annihilates their being. This passage is intensely powerful because its wit is based on an absolutely serious view of the Christian experience of death; in Eliot's words, it 'could not have been written in any other age'. It could not be said of King that he had no myth to sustain his vision.

If the true voice of feeling speaks the language of Revelation, it speaks also in the accents of sardonic Metaphysical wit:

> Mean time, thou hast her, earth: much good
> May my harm do thee. Since it stood
> With Heavens will I might not call
> Her longer mine, I give thee all
> My short-liv'd right and interest

In her, whom living I lov'd best:
With a most free and bounteous grief,
I give thee what I could not keep.
Be kind to her, and prethee look
Thou write into thy Dooms-day book
Each parcell of this Rarity
Which in thy Casket shrin'd doth ly:
See that thou make thy reck'ning streight,
And yield her back again by weight;
For thou must audit on thy trust
Each graine and atome of this dust,
As thou wilt answer *Him* that lent,
Not gave thee, my dear Monument.

So close the ground, and 'bout her shade
Black curtains draw, my *Bride* is laid.

Now the conceits are relentless, the mind recoiling upon its own intelligence. She is of 'earth' now, as he is of earth. They are suspended in the slow orbit of time before their final union. One is 'lov'd clay' already, the other more and more conscious of his own impotence. She is now a 'Rarity', like a jewel in the doubly elusive 'Casket'. She is a 'Monument' in more than one sense, 'this dust', and yet also the '*Bride*', like that of the Persephone legend, whose bright bed is drawn with the 'Black curtains' of earth falling loosely on her coffin. If in the sonnet the beloved assumes the many glowing forms of life, here she is, in more and more somber terms, conceived of as part of the kingdom of death, married to him, weighed on his scales, entered in his book, returned to primal clay.

Her 'cold bed' calls for them both. They are not to flame in 'the forehead of the morning sky', but to meet in the 'hollow Vale' beyond their 'West' of life:

Sleep on my *Love* in thy cold bed
Never to be disquieted!

My last good night! Thou wilt not wake
Till I thy fate shall overtake:
Till age, or grief, or sickness must
Marry my body to that dust
It so much loves; and fill the room
My heart keeps empty in thy Tomb.
Stay for me there; I will not faile
To meet thee in that hollow Vale.
And think not much of my delay;
I am already on the way,
And follow thee with all the speed
Desire can make, or sorrows breed.
Each minute is a short degree,
And ev'ry houre a step towards thee.
At night when I betake to rest,
Next morn I rise neerer my West
Of life, almost by eight houres saile,
Then when sleep breath'd his drowsie gale.

These conceits are disquieting, and they are intended to be
so. As he was paradoxical before, now he writes in the
style of profound and dark burlesque. She 'sleeps' now in
a 'cold bed' beyond the warming, wakening force of
sexual love. She is quiet now, 'never to be disquieted', or
moved by the love of the senses. Their marriage now is
beyond even the fancies of Platonic union, for their next
consummation will be neither of body nor of soul, but dust
to dust, a witty mingling of the marriage sacrament and
the service for the dead. Love and sensuality will not drive
them to embrace, but 'age, or grief, or sickness'. And,
carried by his intelligent wit to a new insight, he sees life
itself as a desirable progress toward its stilled culmination.
There is an unspoken link between death and 'dying'. The
poet conceives of the erotic pun literally – love and death
finally, metaphorically and in reality, fused.

The poem draws to an end with this consciously witty

balancing of life and death. In their equipoise we see the 'effect of terror' remarked by Eliot. The idea of eternity fades, to be replaced by a mordantly imaginative appraisal of death. There is a welded unity in the extended conceit describing the impatient passage of life; there is almost no choice between life and death, one leading perceptibly to the other with the studied loss of vitality and rhythmic march which the verse so admirably reconstructs. Even the pulse, the ultimate sign of life in the beating of the warm blood, is a cold measure of the happy encroachment of death. The 'effect of terror' is understandable, for we have in this one of the most explicit manifestations of the death-wish in Western art. It is an exaggeration of Christian resignation, a morbid, brilliant rendition of the identification of the self with the dead. And underlying it is that sexual love spoken of only indirectly, but which has so much to do with the psychological power of the poem, and which, linked to love of death, is one of the fundamental human enigmas:

> 'Tis true, with shame and grief I yield,
> Thou like the *Vann* first took'st the field,
> And gotten hast the victory
> In thus adventuring to dy
> Before me, whose more years might crave
> A just precedence in the grave.
> But heark! My pulse like a soft Drum
> Beats my approch, tells *Thee* I come;
> And slow howere my marches be,
> I shall at last sit down by *Thee*.

The poem is remarkable if only because of its intimations of man's limits. The persistent use of 'wit' to describe the most intense feeling is itself a limitation; behind each piece of each extended conceit there is an emotion which cannot be completely revealed. The progress from conceit to conceit is relentless. The poem seems to be twisting, seizing, envisioning in any possible way a deprivation which is beyond words. There is a terrible tension between the life of eternity and the real presence of death: part of the poem's power consists of its refusal to artificially reconcile the two elements. This is why the poem has intellectual integrity; rather than sink into the common ritual of eulogy and apotheosis, the poet stands by his recognition that the disharmonies of life are tragic and irrevocable. The poem has only a partially cathartic effect, for its terrible rhythm, its willingness to see life and death with the identical intelligent 'wit' of the conceit, constantly remind us of what awaits beyond life. In many ways the poem is a brilliant attempt at comprehension, like 'In Memoriam'. Like the later poem, it is also a brilliant failure of the mind to ease the spirit.

'Donne *in usum vulgi*'

In Saintsbury's introduction to his edition of King, he remarks that there is a '*via media* of metaphysicality which is King's special path. He is, in fact, a sort of Long-fellow of this particular style and school of poetry – from the other side; a sort of Donne *in usum vulgi*'. This is more in the way of epigram than criticism. While there is in King a good deal of the type of conceit that may have its origin in a lofty aversion to literal expression, we will find also conceit which refines upon Metaphysical technique in a particularly valuable way. To give Saintsbury his due, let us look briefly at a watered-down conceit. In that distinctly Metaphysical genre, the paradox, it exists as a trite expanded metaphor:

> Love is our Reasons Paradox, which still
> Against the judgment doth maintain the Will:
> And governs by such arbitrary laws,

It onely makes the Act our Likings cause:
We have no brave revenge, but to forgo
Our full desires, and starve the Tyrant so.

The visual and sensuous aspects of conceit are missing,
and there is an evident intellectual vacuity. While we
could understand that Love is 'our Reasons Paradox' on
reading the poetry of Donne, we would never be able to
extract the hard, sensuous images of Donne from King's
verse. There is irrelevant logic in King's conceit; we feel
that it is sententious. Suckling was a champion of this
type of conceit, which is amenable to infinite change-
ringing.

King's 'A Letter' goes a long way to demonstrate that
he was something more than a 'Donne *in usum vulgi*'. The
central passage, King's most complex piece of poetry,
contains intricacies of imagery and particularly of verbal
structure which demand careful intellectual appraisal:

Truth be my record, I durst not presume
To seek to you, 'twas you that did assume
Me to your bosom. Wherein you subdu'd
One that can serve you, though ne're could intrude
Upon great titles; nor knows how t'invade
Acquaintance: Like such as are onely paid
With great mens smiles, if that the passant Lord
Let fall a forc't salute, or but afford
The Nod Regardant. It was test enough
For me, you ne're did find such servile stuff
Couch't in my temper; I can freely say,
I do not love you in that common way
For which Great Ones are lov'd in this false time:
I have no wish to gain, nor will to climbe;
I cannot pawn my freedom, nor out-live
My liberty, for all that you can give.
And sure you may retain good cheap such friends,
Who not your fortune make, but you, their ends.

> I speak not this to vaunt in my own story,
> All these additions are unto your glory;
> Who counter to the world use to elect,
> Not to take up on trust what you affect.
> Indeed 'tis seldom seen that such as you
> Adopt a friend, or for acquaintance sue;
> Yet you did this vouchsafe, you did descend
> Below your self, to raise an humble friend,
> And fix him in your love: where I will stand
> The constant subject of your free command.
> Had I no ayerie thoughts, sure you would teach
> Me higher then my own dull sphere to reach:
> And by reflex instruct me to appear
> Something (though course and plain) fit for your wear.

A comment on 'sensable' (as the term is used in
Josephine Miles's *The Continuity of Poetic Language*)
versus 'conceptual' uses of poetry seems applicable here:

> The vocabulary of sense, then, the use of sensable [*sic*] objects
> and qualities as poetic material, defines negatively rather than posi-
> tively the metaphysical school if it is to be centered in Donne,
> Cowley, Vaughan, Carew, Cleveland, and that kind, and repre-
> sents positively the counter or parallel school of Milton, Crashaw,
> Waller, with its emphasis upon image and description. This is not
> to say that sensation and quality were not vivid in the metaphysical
> poets, but to say rather that they were vivid in their individuality,
> particularity, and subordination more than in their consistent poetic
> focus. . . . But their respective choices of poetic substance dis-
> tinctly deviate in terms of a sensuous versus a conceptual medium,
> a descriptive versus a dramatic result.[11]

The 'conceptual' appears to be the mode of this poem. The
thread of argument is intricate, as its condensed antithetical rhetoric is intricate. The jagged, harsh monosyllabic
and dissyllabic language, the irregular rhythm, the total
absence of 'sensable' qualities bespeak verse committed to
the stripped expression of thought. For example, there

are notably few epithets. This is neither bad nor good aesthetically, it simply means that the evocative powers of the epithet are restrained, and that the poem accomplishes its purposes by certain other means. This evocative restraint is figured in the flat, delimited nature of the epithets themselves: 'great', 'servile', 'common'. The qualities of these epithets are of course evocative in a certain sense, but it is in an intellectual rather than 'sensable' mode. 'Great', for example, has sardonic overtones, 'common' has connotations which stretch from the popular or vulgar to the completely prostituted. When, in an epithet like 'ayerie' no special meaning comes readily to mind, there is still an abstract limitation to its usage.

Restraint is figured also in sparsity; it is only in the fifth line that the first adjective occurs, in 'great titles'. After that the sardonic 'passant Lord' and 'Nod Regardant', carefully coined adjectival phrases, economically describe while they belittle. Thereafter adjectives are uncompromising in meaning, harsh in effect. We find in certain lines the single adjectival phrase taking the burden of characterization, hammering out the quality aimed at by the poet:

> It was test enough
> For me, you ne're did find such servile stuff
> Couch't in my temper.

> I do not love you in that common way
> For which Great Ones are lov'd in this false time.

> Had I no ayerie thoughts, sure you would teach
> Me higher then my own dull sphere to reach.

The verbal structure is the core of the passage. Its tight antithetical patterns and subtleties of definition give the poem a tone of extreme intellectuality. While the rhetoric is in dramatic form, and might even appear spontaneous (what Miss Miles calls 'the tone and structure of talk'), there is a Metaphysical habit of ingenuity and even of premeditation which forces the mind to perceive the poem in terms of 'wit' rather than in any other way.

The strangely ceremonial language and logic are enough removed from 'the tone and structure of talk' to make us aware that some kind of meaning in addition to that figured may be present. We see not only a description of friendship, but the complex, introspective character of the 'persona', the recurrent 'incorruptible poet' of his poetry. The angry note of satire, which continually appears in this poem, impels it even from the first lines:

> I ne'r was drest in Forms; nor can I bend
> My pen to flatter any, nor commend,
> Unless desert or honour do present
> Unto my verse a worthy argument.

This is a satirical poem in two senses. The one, against literary time-servers (like Juvenal's Satire *III*, 'Quid quod adulandi gens prudentissima . . .'), is fairly evident. We may note King's comments in this vein in 'To his Unconstant Friend' and 'By occasion of the Young Prince his happy birth', discussed above. In a second and less evident manner the poem criticizes that debased verse which is also 'drest in Forms'. King condemns the great body of verse which, in the most superficial terms, attempts to express an idea. This type of poetry reveals nothing of the workings of intelligence, but contents itself with platitudes. Tied to convention, it is the natural enemy of artistry. Juvenal's poet of Satire *VII* was to be the model for the intellectual poets of the Renaissance:

> vatem egregium, cui non sit publica vena,
> qui nil expositum soleat deducere nec qui
> communi feriat carmen triviale moneta. . . .

Carew's criticism of 'servile imitation' in his elegy on Donne is well-known, and Lord Herbert's is equally contemptuous. He too bitterly complains of 'Those common words which men may even rake / From dunghill-wits'. King's poem seems to be in this tradition, both in his explicit rejection of 'Forms', and in his implicit dependence on the reformed verse introduced by Donne.

By putting away the glowing vocabulary which has been so well tabulated in *The Continuity of Poetic Language* the poet strives for precise responses. King's opening lines, like Bolingbroke's opening words in *Richard II*, invoke a ceremony of honesty. The poetry is largely moral, an acknowledgment (''twas you that did assume / Me to your bosom,') of spiritual obligation. The images are strongly physical:

> Wherein you subdu'd
> One that can serve you, though ne're could intrude
> Upon great titles; nor knows how t'invade
> Acquaintance.

They delineate the force of the conquest of one incorruptible man by another. The heraldic images of 'the passant Lord' and 'the Nod Regardant' are more than minor masterpieces of condensation. Their languid, effeminate passivity is in strong contrast to the vigor of the preceding lines, where virtue is actively figured in the sharp transitive verbs. Virtue is, in one sense, action. There is a burst of short, active verbs:

> I have no wish to gain, nor will to climbe;
> I cannot pawn my freedom, nor out-live
> My liberty, for all that you can give.

This deliberately underscores the unaffected, Jonsonian speech of the man of virtue. The concluding lines juggle

131

purely colloquial terms ('And sure you may retain good cheap such friends') and elevated language which gains unaccustomed strength. In the concluding quatrain King's relationship to Donne is plainest, in his use of conceit and diction which insist on transposing the objects of verse from ideal and esoteric images to solidly physical ones:

> Had I no ayerie thoughts, sure you would teach
> Me higher then my own dull sphere to reach:
> And by reflex instruct me to appear
> Something (though course and plain) fit for your wear.

The Metaphysical peripeteia of this quatrain, like that of the whole passage, is the vehicle for the poet's delineation of the process of thought. His perception of his own intellectual and spiritual subordination is the basis for the antithesis between his own limitations and the other's transcendence. But the movement of the quatrain is not confined to the statement of a perception and the formation of an antithesis. The delicate praise of the first couplet is condensed in the wit of the following line, in which the idea of teaching necessitates only the brilliance of reflection. The impersonal nature of this line is radically confronted by the concrete, even coarse nature of the last. From the original perception of contrast, through the 'witty' idea of learning, evolves the suddenly appropriate visual image which will define the relationship of the two. The progress from idea to image reveals the shifting, vital insight of the poet, belying his modesty.

The masculine simplicity of King's rhetoric at its best may easily allow it to be underrated. While his diction, like Donne's, may be recondite and ambiguous, it may also, like Dryden's, be chosen for perspicuity. Probably no poem reveals a deliberate masculinity so much as his elegy, 'To my dead friend Ben: Johnson'. As he used passionate conceited terms in his elegy on Donne, he uses a reflective and harsh series of concrete terms for Jonson:

> For 'tis but truth; thou taught'st the ruder age
> To speake by Grammar, and reform'dst the Stage:
> Thy Comick Sock induc'd such purged sence,
> A *Lucrece* might have heard without offence.
> Amongst those soaring wits that did dilate
> Our English, and advance it to the rate
> And value it now holds, thy self was one
> Helpt lift it up to such proportion,
> That thus refin'd and roab'd, it shall not spare
> With the full *Greek* or *Latine* to compare.

*   *   *   *   *

> All I would ask for thee, in recompence
> Of thy successful toyl and times expence,
> Is onely this poor Boon: that those who can
> Perhaps read *French*, or talk *Italian*,
> Or do the lofty *Spaniard* affect,
> (To shew their skill in Forrein Dialect)
> Prove not themselves so unnaturally wise,
> They therefore should their *Mother-tongue* despise
> (As if her Poets both for style and wit
> Not equall'd, or not pass'd their best that writ)
> Untill by studying *Johnson* they have known
> The height and strength and plenty of their own.

King's manner imitates the Jonsonian, as his criticism praises it. There are many hard syllables, monosyllabic and dissyllabic words, and sharp contrasts of Latin-derived and Anglo-Saxon diction. His last couplet condenses these characteristics remarkably. There is a unique ambiguousness to the three terms of the last line; they seem to point to definitive qualities of the Jonsonian verse, as well as to certain indefinable ideas on the nature of language.

King's 'reformed' rhetoric seems to lend these very

qualities to the series of conceits with which his poem closes. They are not 'strong-lin'd'; instead, they fulfil Jonson's Horation demand:

> Him, whose choice doth reare
> His matter to his power, in all he makes,
> Nor language, nor cleere order ere forsakes.
> The vertue of which order, and true grace
> Or I am much deceiv'd, shall be to place
> Invention.[12]

King is restrained in his work by this formula:

> Thus in what low earth or neglected room
> Soere thou sleep'st, *thy book* shall be thy tomb.
> Thou wilt go down a happy Coarse, bestrew'd
> With thine own Flowres; and feel thy self renew'd,
> Whil'st thy immortal never-with'ring Bayes
> Shall yearly flourish in thy Readers praise.
> And when more spreading Titles are forgot,
> Or, spight of all their Lead and Sear-cloth, rot,
> Thou, wrapt and Shrin'd in *thine own sheets*, wilt ly
> A Relick fam'd by all Posterity.

In Jasper Mayne's overgrown elegy on Jonson, also printed in *Jonsonus Virbius*, there is no tightness, no unity in the collection of conceits. While King, the poet who 'nor cleere order ere forsakes', follows the track of his thoughts with a certain discipline, Mayne's verse typifies the indiscriminate and indecorous possibilities of the conceit:

> *Thou'lt* have a whole *Name* still, nor needst *thou* feare
> *That* will be ruin'd, or lose *nose*, or *haire*.[13]

A summation of King's poetry is difficult, perhaps not really possible. While he revealed strong Jonsonian and Donnian traits, certain of his poems like 'A Letter' and 'The Exequy' display traits peculiarly his own. They are obstinately rational: in the latter poem he refuses the comforting logic of the meditation tradition, and answers his own grief with a sardonic conceit:

> So close the ground, and 'bout her shade
> Black curtains draw, my *Bride* is laid.

While he was, in lesser poems, obsessed with ephemera, he was in his major work intensely critical of that indiscriminate adherence to a convention which results merely in poetry of the 'stock response'. Whether we consider his overt use of the 'persona' of the 'incorruptible poet' or his less obvious ironic variations on the motif, we can perceive the method of his rationality. Each considered variation of imagery and conceit, each twist of antithetical logic, marks the mind for whom intelligence is a primary element of poetry.

APPENDIX

ANTHOLOGY SELECTIONS OF
HENRY KING'S POETRY

ANTHOLOGISTS from the late eighteenth to the early twentieth century seem to have confused 'sublimity' with melancholy, and what may well have been *jeux d'esprit* with profundity. A standard canon of King's works evolved, consisting almost solely of 'The Dirge' and 'Sic Vita', both charming but trifling poems. Their cultivated pathos, however, seems to have satisfied the time, and King became known as a sincerely emotional, moral, and sentimental poet. Funereal morality was perhaps as popular as in the time of James I, but it was rather more shallow: the public, at any rate, was not confronted with King's satirical complexity.

Headley, Henry, ed., *Select Beauties of Ancient English Poetry*, 2 vols. (London, 1787).
    'My Midnight Meditation'
    'Sic Vita'
    'The Exequy'
    'The Surrender'
    'The Legacy'
    'Dry those fair, those chrystal eyes'

Ellis, George, ed., *Specimens of the Early English Poets*, 3 vols. (London, 1845). First edition 1790.
    'The Dirge'
    'The Surrender'
    'To Patience'

Ritson, Joseph, ed., *The English Anthology*, 3 vols. (London, 1793-4).
    'The Farewell'

Campbell, Thomas, ed., *Specimens of the British Poets*, 7 vols. (London, 1819).
   'The Dirge'
   'Sic Vita'
   'Dry those fair, those chrystal eyes'

Mitford, John, ed., *Sacred Specimens from the Early English Poets* (London, 1827).
   'The Dirge'

Halleck, Fitz-Greene, ed., *Selections from the British Poets*, 2 vols. (New York, 1840).
   'Sic Vita'
   'The Dirge'

Griswold, Rufus, ed., *The Sacred Poets of England and America* (New York, 1850).
   'Sic Vita'
   'The Dirge'
   'The Anniversary'

Rossetti, W. M. and Beeton, S. O., eds., *The Encyclopaedia of English and American Poetry* (London, 1873).
   'Sic Vita‚
   'The Dirge'
   'Dry those fair, those chrystal eyes'

Bailey, John Cann, ed., *English Elegies* (London, 1900).
   'The Exequy'

NOTES

Chapter I: The Man

1. James Howell, *Familiar Letters*, ed. J. Jacob (London, 1892), II, 406.

2. Izaak Walton, *The Compleat Walton*, ed. Geoffrey Keynes (London, 1929), pp. 596-97.

3. Henry King, 'To my Sister Anne King, who chid me in verse for being angry', *The Poems of Bishop Henry King*, ed. J. Sparrow (London, 1925), p. 58.

4. *Vide* Percy Simpson's article, 'John and Henry King: A Correction', *Bodleian Library Record*, IV (1952-53), 208. *Vide* also the original article by Simpson, on which the above is based: 'The Bodleian Manuscripts of Henry King', *Bodleian Quarterly Record*, V (1926-28), 324 ff.

5. James Howell, *Familiar Letters*, *loc. cit.*

6. 'King James... commonly called him "the King of preachers". And Sir Edward Coke would say of him, "he was the best speaker in Star Chamber in his time".' Thomas Fuller, *The Church History of Britain*, ed. J. S. Brewer (Oxford, 1845), V, 499.

7. Lawrence Mason, 'The Life and Works of Henry King, D. D.', *Transactions of the Connecticut Academy of Arts and Sciences*, XVIII (November, 1913), 229.

8. Henry King, *A Sermon Preached at the Funeral of the R' Reverend Father in God Bryan, Lord Bp. of Winchester* (London, 1662), p. 34.

9. Lawrence Mason, 'The Life and Works of Henry King, D.D.', *Transactions . . .* , XVIII, 232.

10. *Vide* the Preface to *The Poems of Richard Corbett*, ed. J. A. W. Bennett and H. R. Trevor-Roper (Oxford, 1955).

11. Lawrence Mason, 'The Life and Works of Henry King, D.D.', *Transactions* . . . , XVIII, 231.

12. John Chamberlain to Sir Dudley Carleton, November 8, 1617: *vide* John Nichols, *The Progresses, Processions, and Magnificent Festivities of King James I* (London, 1828), III, 445.

13. Izaak Walton, 'The Life of Dr. John Donne', *Lives* (Oxford, 1950), p. 47.

14. Izaak Walton, Dedication to Sir Robert Holt of Aston, *The Life of John Donne* (London, 1658).

15. Izaak Walton, *Lives*, p. 78.

16. Cf. Sir Edmund Gosse, *The Life and Letters of John Donne* (New York, 1899), II, 187-88, 298-300, 308, 360; *The Sermons of John Donne*, ed. E. M. Simpson and G. R. Potter (Berkeley, Calif., 1953), I, 1, 46-47; *The Poems of John Donne*, ed. Sir Herbert Grierson (Oxford, 1953), II, lxvi, 255; *Poems and Psalms by Henry King D.D.*, ed. J. Hannah (Oxford, 1843), pp. xxix ff.

17. Edward, Earl of Clarendon, *The History of the Rebellion and Civil Wars in England*, ed. W. D. MacRay (Oxford, 1888), I, 401. First edition 1702-04.

18. William Prynne, *The Antipathie of the English Lordly Prelacie, Both to Regall Monarchy, and Civill Unity* (London, 1641), p. 505.

19. Bruno Ryves, *Mercurius Rusticus: or, The Countries Complaint of the Sacriledges, Prophanations, and Plunderings, Committed by the Schismatiques on the Cathedrall Churches of this Kingdome* (Oxford, 1646), pp. 202-06.

20. *Poems and Psalms by Henry King D.D.*, p. cix.

21. John Walker, *An Attempt Towards Recovering an Account of the Numbers and Sufferings of the Clergy of the Church of England* (London, 1714), Part II, 11. *Vide* Mason, 'The Life and Works of Henry King, D.D.', *Transactions* . . . , XVIII, 240-41.

22. Henry King, 'A Deepe Groane', *The Poems of Bishop Henry King*, p. 136.

23. George Saintsbury, ed., *Minor Poets of the Caroline Period* (Oxford, 1921), III, 164n.

24. Samuel Woodford, Preface, *A Paraphrase upon the Psalms of David* (London, 1667).

25. Edward Phillips, *Theatrum Poetarum Anglicanorum*, ed. Sir E. Brydges (Geneva, 1824), II, 17. First edition 1675.

26. John Patrick, *Century of Select Psalms*. Quoted in Hannah's edition of King, p. 217. First edition 1679.

27. Payne Fisher, ed., Dedication to Bishop King, *Poems on Several Choice and Various Subjects, Occasionally Composed by an Eminent Author* (London, 1663).

28. Henry King, *A Sermon Preached at the Funeral of . . . Lord Bp. of Winchester*, pp. 41 ff. *Vide* Sir Gyles Isham, *The Correspondence of Bishop Brian Duppa and Sir Justinian Isham* (Northampton, England, 1955), p. 165.

29. Samuel Pepys, *Diary*, ed. H. B. Wheatley (London, 1924), I, 181; III, 58; IV, 346 – entries of July 8, 1660; March 8, 1662-63; March 12, 1664-65.

30. W. R. W. Stephens, *Diocesan Histories, the South Saxon Diocese, Selsey-Chichester* (London, 1881), pp. 226-27.

31. Tanner MS., xlv, fol. 64, Bodleian library. *Vide* Percy Simpson, 'The Bodleian Manuscripts of Henry King', *Bodleian Quarterly Record*, V, 338.

32. R. W. Blencowe, 'Paxhill and its Neighborhood', *Sussex Archaeological Collections*, XI (1859), 33. Wood and Le Neve (*Fasti Ecclesiae Anglicanae*) state that Dr Frewen was translated in October, 1660; Dr Burton died in 1661.

33. Thomas Fuller, *The Worthies of England*, ed. J. Freeman (London, 1952), p. 44. First edition 1662.

34. Anthony à Wood, *Athenae Oxonienses*, ed. P. Bliss (London, 1817), III, 839. First edition 1691-92. William Winstanley, *The Lives of the Most Famous English Poets, or the Honour of Parnassus* (London, 1687), pp. 202-4. White Kennett, Lord Bishop of Peterborough, *A Register and Chronicle Ecclesiastical and Civil* (London, 1728), p. 650. Giles Jacob, *An Historical Account of the Lives and Writings*

of our most considerable English Poets, whether Epick, Lyrick, Elegiack, Epigrammatists, etc. (London, 1720), II, 86.

35. Thomas Zouch, *The Life of Izaak Walton* (London, 1823), p. 13.

36. *Ibid.*, p. 12.

37. These were edited by Lawrence Mason (1914), George Saintsbury (1921), and John Sparrow (1925).

Chapter II: Henry King and his Milieu

1. (1559-1621) Educated at Westminster and Oxford. He took the B.A. in 1579-80, and the M.A. in 1582-83. He received the D.D. in 1601, when well along in his ecclesiastical career. Archdeacon of Nottingham in 1590, and, by 1594, Chaplain to Sir Thomas Egerton, Lord Keeper. Dean of Christ Church, Oxford, in 1605, and Vice-Chancellor of the University from 1607 to 1610. Bishop of London from 1611 until his death in 1621.

2. 1612.

3. Thomas Fuller, *The Church History of Britain*, ed. J. S. Brewer (Oxford, 1845), V, 419-23.

4. William Haller, *The Rise of Puritanism* (New York, 1938), p. 49.

5. 'A Narration of the Burning of Bartholomew Legatt', in *Truth brought to light and discovered by time, or a Discourse and Historical Narration of the first XIIII yeares of King Iames Reigne* (London, 1651), p. 6.

6. Michael Servetus, born in 1511, in Spain. After an early career of orthodoxy, he quarreled with prevalent Protestant ideas on the Trinity (*De Trinitatis erroribus*, 1531). Like Legate, but with considerably more learning, he denied the divinity of Christ. He entered into a controversy with Calvin and published *Christianismi restitutio*, which was declared heretical at his trial in Geneva in 1553. He was burned immediately after his trial.

7. R. N. C. Hunt, *Calvin* (London, 1933), pp. 218-19.

8. Henry King, *A Sermon Preached at the Funeral of the R'Reverend Father in God Bryan, Lord Bp. of Winchester* (London, 1662), p. 28.

9. Richard Hooker, *Of the Laws of Ecclesiastical Polity,* (London, 1954), I, 135.

10. John King, *The Fourth Sermon Preached at Hampton Court on Tuesday the last of Sept. 1606* (Oxford, 1606), p. 3.

11. *Ibid.,* pp. 4-5.

12. *Ibid.,* p. 17.

13. *Ibid.,* p. 25.

14. Henry King, *A Sermon Preached at St. Pauls March 27. 1640* (London, 1640), p. 6.

15. John King, *The Fourth Sermon Preached at Hampton Court . . . Sept. 1606,* p. 45.

16. Richard Hooker, *Of the Laws of Ecclesiastical Polity,* I, 96-97.

17. Lancelot Andrewes, 'A Sermon Preached Before the King's Majesty at Rumsey, on the Fifth of August, A.D. MDCVII', *Ninety-Six Sermons,* ed. J. P. Wilson (Oxford, 1841), IV, 11, 12.

18. Henry King, *A Sermon Preached at St. Pauls March 27. 1640,* pp. 14-16.

19. John Donne, *Essayes in Divinity* (London, 1651), p. 110.

20. *Ibid.,* pp. 104-6.

21. Henry King, *A Sermon Preached at St. Pauls March 27. 1640,* pp. 19-20.

22. John Elliott, *The Christian Commonwealth* (1660). Quoted in Reinhold Niebuhr's *Faith and History* (New York, 1951), p. 204.

23. John Donne, 'Psalms 38.4', *Sermons,* ed. E. M. Simpson and G. R. Potter (Berkeley, 1955), II, 112-13. Cf. R. A. Knox, *Enthusiasm* (Oxford, 1957), p. 3: 'The saved man has come out into a new order of being, with a new set of faculties which are proper to his state. . . . A direct indication of the Divine Will is communicated to him at every turn.'

24. John Donne, *Essayes in Divinity*, p. 190.

25. John Donne, *Sermons*, II, 379. This is an early version of 'Eccles. 12.1'.

26. John Donne, 'Colos. 1.24.', *Sermons*, III (1957), 338.

27. Henry King, *A Sermon Preached at Pauls Crosse, the 25. of November. 1621* (London, 1621), p. 5.

28. Henry King, *A Sermon Preached at St. Pauls March 27. 1640*, p. 48.

29. Henry King, *An Exposition Upon the Lords Prayer* (London, 1628), pp. 13-14.

30. Thomas Fuller, *The Church History of Britain*, V, 559.

31. John Donne, *LXXX Sermons* (London, 1640), pp. 671-72.

32. Henry King, *A Sermon of Deliverance* (London, 1626), p. 12.

33. John Pearson, quoted in James Elson, *John Hales of Eton* (New York, 1948), p. 7.

34. John Hales, 'Abuses of Hard Places of Scripture', in *Works*, ed. D. Dalrymple, 3 vols. (Glasgow, 1765), II, 4.

35. *Ibid.*, II, 17.

36. Henry King, *A Sermon Preached at Lewis in the Diocess of Chichester* (London, 1663), p. 25.

37. John Hales, 'Abuses of Hard Places of Scripture', in *Works*, II, 28.

38. John Hales, 'A Tract on the Sacrament of the Lord's Supper', in *Works*, I, 68.

39. George Fox, *Journal*, ed. Thomas Ellwood (London, 1694), p. 169.

40. *Ibid.*, p. 89.

41. Margaret Cavendish, Duchess of Newcastle, 'A Conventicle', in *The Cavalier and his Lady*, ed. Edward Jenkins (London, 1872), pp. 273-75.

42. John Hales, 'Abuses of Hard Places of Scripture', in *Works*, II, 40-41.

43. John Hales, 'A Tract Concerning Schism and Schismatics', in *Works*, I, 114.

44. John Hales, 'A Letter to Archbishop Laud', in *Works*, I, 142.

Chapter III: Degree, Priority, and Place

1. Henry King, *A Sermon Preached at Pauls Crosse, the 25. of November. 1621* (London, 1621), p. 25.

2. Henry King, *A Sermon of Deliverance* (London, 1626), pp. 4-5.

3. M. M. Mahood, *Poetry and Humanism* (London, 1950), p. 190.

4. Henry King, *A Sermon Preached at St. Pauls March 27. 1640* (London, 1640), p. 14.

5. *Ibid.*, p. 29.

6. *Ibid.*, p. 39.

7. *Ibid.*, p. 19.

8. Henry King, *A Sermon of Deliverance*, p. 56.

9. Henry King, *A Sermon Preached at White-Hall on the 29th. of May* (London, 1661), pp. 19-23.

10. *Ibid.*, pp. 26-28. Buchanan's *De Jure Regni Apud Scotos* shared with the work of Mariana the distinction of being most odious to the orthodoxy of James I.

11. Henry King, *A Sermon Preached at White-Hall on the 29th. of May*, p. 24. Like Filmer, King conceived of a monarch, 'Omnes sub Eo & Ipse sub nullo, nisi tantum sub Deo' (*Patriarcha*).

12. Henry King, *A Sermon Preached the 30th of January at White-Hall, 1664* (London, 1665), p. 15.

13. Henry King, *A Sermon Preached at St. Pauls March 27. 1640*, pp. 30-31.

14. *Ibid.*, pp. 29-30.

15. King James I, *The Political Works*, ed. C. H. McIlwain (Cambridge, Mass., 1918), p. 12.

16. *Ibid.*, p. 54.

17. *Ibid.*, p. 64.

18. *Ibid.*, p. 272.

19. Henry King, *A Sermon Preached at White-Hall on the 29th. of May*, p. 9.

20. Henry King, *A Sermon Preached at Pauls Crosse the 25. of November. 1621*, p. 5.

21. Henry King, *A Sermon Preached at Pauls Crosse the 25. of November, 1621*, p. 5.
22. Henry King, *A Sermon Preached at the Funeral of the R'Reverend Father in God Bryan, Lord Bp. of Winchester* (London, 1662), p. 21.
23. Henry King, *A Sermon Preached the 30th of January at White-Hall, 1664*, p. 4.
24. *Ibid.*, p. 34.

Chapter IV: Words of Truth and Soberness

1. W. Fraser Mitchell, *English Pulpit Oratory from Andrewes to Tillotson* (London, 1932), p. 118. From Samuel Clarke, *The Lives of Thirty-Two English Divines* (London, 1677), p. 64.
2. Henry King, *A Sermon Preached at Lewis in the Diocess of Chichester* (London, 1663), p. 18.
3. Robert South, 'A Sermon Preached at Christ-Church, Oxon, on the 30th of April, 1668', in *Sermons Preached Upon Several Occasions* (Oxford, 1842), III, 319-20.
4. Henry King, *A Sermon Preached at Lewis in the Diocess of Chichester*, p. 24.
5. *Ibid.*, pp. 25-26.
6. Samuel Butler, *Satires and Miscellaneous Poetry and Prose*, ed. R. Lamar (Cambridge, England, 1928), p. 90.
7. Henry King, *A Sermon Preached at Lewis in the Diocess of Chichester*, p. 21.
8. *Ibid.*, p. 38.
9. Izaak Walton, 'The Life of Dr. Sanderson', in *Lives* (Oxford, 1950), pp. 397-98.
10. Henry King, 'David's Enlargement', *Two Sermons. Upon the Act Sunday, Being the 10th of July. 1625* (Oxford, 1625), pp. 1-2.
11. M. M. Mahood, *Poetry and Humanism* (London, 1950), p. 142.
12. Henry King, 'David's Enlargement', *Two Sermons . . .*, pp. 19-20.

13. Henry King, *A Sermon Preached at St. Pauls March 27. 1640* (London, 1640), pp. 32-34.

14. Joseph Glanvill, 'An Essay Concerning Preaching', in *Critical Essays of the Seventeenth Century*, ed. J. E. Spingarn, (Bloomington, 1957), II, 276.

15. Henry King, *A Sermon Preached the 30th of January at White-Hall, 1664* (London, 1665), p. 8.

16. *Ibid.*, p. 43.

17. *Ibid.*, p. 44.

18. Joseph Glanvill, 'A Fast Sermon on the King's Martyrdom', in *Some Discourses, Sermons and Remains of the Reverend Mr. Jos. Glanvil* (London, 1681), pp. 152-53.

19. Henry King, *A Sermon Preached at White-Hall in Lent. 1625* (London, 1627), pp. 7-8.

20. *Ibid.*, p. 15.

21. *Ibid.*, pp. 16-17.

22. Henry King, *A Sermon Preached at Pauls Crosse, the 25. of November. 1621* (London, 1621), p. 35.

23. Joseph Glanvill, 'A Fast Sermon on the King's Martyrdom', *Some Discourses . . .* , pp. 176-77.

24. Henry King, *A Sermon Preached at St. Pauls March 27. 1640*, p. 19.

25. *Ibid.*, p. 16.

26. *Ibid.*, p. 14.

27. *Ibid.*, p. 49.

28. John Tillotson, 'Of the Education of Children', *Sermons on Severall Subjects and Occasions* (London, 1742), IV, 515.

29. W. K. Wimsatt, Jr., *The Prose Style of Samuel Johnson* (New Haven, 1941), p. 47.

30. Henry King, *A Sermon Preached at the Funeral of the R'Reverend Father in God Bryan, Lord Bp. of Winchester* (London, 1662), p. 2.

31. *Ibid.*

32. Henry King, *A Sermon Preached the 30th of January at White-Hall, 1664*, p. 4.

33. Henry King, *A Sermon Preached the 30th of January at White-Hall*, 1664, p. 6.

34. *Ibid.*, p. 17.

35. *Ibid.*, pp. 43-44.

36. Henry King, *A Sermon Preached at Lewis in the Diocessſo Chichester*, p. 6.

37. *Ibid.*, p. 37.

Chapter V: The Noble Art

1. Henry W. Foote, *Three Centuries of American Hymnody* (Cambridge, Mass., 1940), p. 24.

2. Thomas Fuller, *The Church History of Britain*, ed. J. S. Brewer (Oxford, 1845), IV, 73-74.

3. William Barton, *The Book of Psalms in Metre. Close and Proper to the Hebrew* (London, 1682), pp. vii-viii.

4. *Ibid.*, p. ix.

5. *Ibid.*

6. Simon Ford, *A New Version of the Psalms of David* (London, 1688), p. vi.

7. *Ibid.*

8. *Ibid.*, p. viii.

9. *Ibid.*, p. xiii.

10. *Ibid.*, pp. xxvii-xxviii.

11. Abraham Cowley, 'The Preface to the Poems, 1656', in *The Essays and Other Prose Writings*, ed. A. B. Gough (Oxford, 1915), pp. 16-17.

12. Sir Philip Sidney, *Works*, ed. A. Feuillerat (Cambridge, England, 1923), III, 200.

13. *The Psalmists of Britain*, ed. John Holland (London, 1843), I, 286.

14. Richard Crashaw, *Poems*, ed. L. C. Martin (Oxford, 1957), pp. 102-04.

15. Psalm *LXVIII*, quoted in Foote, *Three Centuries of American Hymnody*, p. 17.

16. Henry Ainsworth, *Annotations Upon the Book of Psalmes and the Psalms in Metre* (Amsterdam, 1617), Psalm *XXVI*.

17. P. Von Rohr-Sauer, *English Metrical Psalms from 1600-1660* (Freiburg, 1938), p. 38. I am heavily in debt to the author's scholarship. R. B.

18. *Ibid.* 'Baxter sought to write many of his psalms so that they could be sung in two metres. He did this by bracketing certain words. Thus LM could be sung as CM or CM as short metre. But his unique innovation was far from successful, for Baxter's muse had difficulty enough in writing the most elementary verse, let alone such experiments.'

19. P. Von Rohr-Sauer, *English Metrical Psalms from 1600-1660*, p. 24. 'Unfortunately Dod's psalms are no better than his rhymed version of Parliament's act enjoining a public thanksgiving for November 5.'

20. John Stoughton, 'The Church of the Restoration', in *Ecclesiastical History of England* (London, 1870), IV, 466-67.

21. Francis Rous issued his *Psalms* in 1641, William Barton published his translation in 1644. Either one would fit (King's) description of a zealous and vulgar translator.

22. *Poems and Psalms by Henry King D.D.*, ed. J. Hannah (Oxford, 1843), p. 139.

23. Henry King, *The Psalmes of David* . . . (London, 1651), p. ii.

24. *Ibid.*, p. iii.

25. John Patrick, *Century of Select Psalms* quoted in Hannah's edition of King, p. 217. First edition 1679.

26. Henry King, *The Psalmes of David* . . . , p. 34.

27. *Ibid.*, p. 89.

28. *Ibid.*, pp. 169-70.

29. *Ibid.*, p. 207.

30. William Barton, *The Book of Psalms* . . . , p. 298.

31. Henry King, Psalm *CXXXIX*, *The Psalmes of David* . . . , p. 267.

32. William Barton, *The Book of Psalms* . . . , p. 380.

33. Henry King, *The Psalmes of David* . . . , pp. 140-41.

Chapter VI: Poetry and the Tradition

1. Robert Penn Warren, 'Pure and Impure Poetry', *Critiques and Essays in Criticism*, ed. R. Stallman (New York, 1949), pp. 85-104.

2. Henry King, *The Poems of Bishop Henry King*, ed. J. Sparrow (London, 1925), p. 3. All of King's poetry reproduced in this chapter is from this edition.

3. T. S. Eliot, 'Whispers of Immortality', in *The Complete Poems and Plays* (New York, 1952), pp. 32-33.

4. R. Wallerstein, *Studies in Seventeenth-Century Poetic* (Madison, Wis., 1950), p. 68.

5. Thomas Carew, 'In answer of an Elegiacall Letter upon the death of the King of Sweden from Aurelian Townsend, inviting me to write on that subject,' in *Poems* (Oxford, 1957), p. 77.

6. *Vide* Appendix.

7. Henry King, 'The Labyrinth', in *The Poems of Bishop Henry King*, p. 91.

8. Henry King, 'My Midnight Meditation', *ibid.*, p. 94.

9. Louis Martz, *The Poetry of Meditation* (New Haven, Conn., 1954), pp. 135-36. Quoted from Fray Luis de Granada, *Of Prayer, and Meditation*, trans. Richard Hopkins (1612), pp. 203-4.

10. Henry King, *A Sermon Preached at the Funeral of the R'Reverend Father in God Bryan, Lord Bp. of Winchester* (London, 1662), p. 2.

11. Josephine Miles, *The Continuity of Poetic Language* (Berkeley, Calif., 1951), pp. 131-32.

12. Ben Jonson, 'Horace, Of the Art of Poetrie', in *Works*, ed. C. H. Herford, P. Simpson, and E. M. Simpson, (Oxford, 1954), VIII, 307.

13. Ben Jonson, *Works*, XI, 452.

BIBLIOGRAPHY

Works of Henry King*

POEMS

Elegy upon K. Charles I (1649).

A Groane at the Funerall of Charles the First (1649).

A Deepe Groane (1649).

Poems, Elegies, Paradoxes, and Sonnets (London, 1657).

Poems, Elegies, Paradoxes, And Sonets (London, 1664).

Ben Johnson's Poems, Elegies, Paradoxes, and Sonnets (London, 1700).

Poems and Psalms by Henry King D.D., ed. J. Hannah (Oxford, 1843).

The English Poems of Henry King, D.D., ed. L. Mason (New Haven, 1914).

Minor Poets of the Caroline Period, ed. G. Saintsbury, 3 vols. (Oxford, 1921).

The Poems of Bishop Henry King, ed. J. Sparrow (London, 1925).

Poems of Bishop Henry King, ed. James R. Baker (Denver, 1960).

PSALMS

The Psalmes of David, from the New Translation of the Bible Turned into Meter (London, 1651).

The Psalmes of David, . . . Unto which are newly added the Lord's Prayer, the Creed, the ten Commandements (London, 1654).

The Psalms of David, from the New Translation of the Bible Turned into Meter (London, 1671).

Poems and Psalms by Henry King D.D., ed. J. Hannah (Oxford, 1843).

* For extended bibliographical discussion see Lawrence Mason, 'The Life and Works of Henry King, D.D.', *Transactions of the Connecticut Academy of Arts and Sciences*, XVIII (November, 1913), 260 ff.

SERMONS

A Sermon Preached at Pauls Crosse, the 25. of November. 1621 (London, 1621).

'David's Enlargement', *Two Sermons. Upon the Act Sunday, Being the 10th of Iuly. 1625* (Oxford, 1625).

A Sermon of Deliverance (London, 1626).

Two Sermons Preached at White-Hall in Lent, March 3. 1625. And Februarie 20. 1626 (London, 1627).

An Exposition upon The Lords Prayer (London, 1628).

An Exposition upon the Lords Prayer (London, 1634).

A Sermon Preached at St. Pauls March 27. 1640 (London, 1640).

A Sermon Preached at White-Hall on the 29th of May (London, 1661).

A Sermon Preached at the Funeral of the R' Reverend Father in God Bryan, Lord Bp. of Winchester (London, 1662).

A Sermon Preached at Lewis in the Diocess of Chichester (London 1663).

A Sermon Preached the 30th of January at White-Hall, 1664 (London, 1665).

A Sermon preached at White-Hall On the 29th of May, 1661 (London, 1713).

LETTERS

To Mr Powell, dated Dec. 13, 1639. First printed in Hannah, pp. xxxviii-xxxix. Reprinted in Lawrence Mason, 'The Life and Works of Henry King, D.D.', *Transactions of the Connecticut Academy of Arts and Sciences*, XVIII (November, 1913), 288.

To Archbishop Ussher, dated Oct. 30, 1651. First printed as letter cclxv in Richard Parr's *Life of . . . Usher* (1686). Reprinted in *Poems and Psalms by Henry King D.D.*, ed. J. Hannah (Oxford, 1843), pp. 138-40.

To Edward Bysshe, dated Jan. 22, 1656. First printed in *The Life, Diary, and Correspondence of Sir William Dugdale*, ed. W. Hamper (London, 1827), pp. 317-18. Reprinted in Mason, 'The Life and Works of Henry King, D.D.', *Transactions . . .* , XVIII, 287-88.

To Izaak Walton, dated Nov. 17, 1664. First printed with Walton's *Life of Hooker*, 1665. Reprinted in *Lives* (Oxford, 1927).

To Gilbert Sheldon, Archbishop of Canterbury, dated Feb. 21, 1666. Tanner MS., xlv, fol. 64, Bodleian library. Described in Percy Simpson, 'The Bodleian Manuscripts of Henry King', *Bodleian Quarterly Record*, V (1926-28), 338.

To Gilbert Sheldon, Archbishop of Canterbury, dated April 23, 1666. Tanner MS., xlv, fol. 73, Bodleian library. Printed in Mason, 'The Life and Works of Henry King, D.D.', *Transactions* . . . , XVIII, 289.

To Gilbert Sheldon, Archbishop of Canterbury, dated Feb. 3, 1668. Tanner MS., xliv, fol. 80, Bodleian library. Printed in Mason, 'The Life and Works of Henry King, D.D.', *Transactions* . . . , XVIII, 289.

To Gilbert Sheldon, Archbishop of Canterbury, dated July 23, 1668. Tanner MS., xliv, fol. 20. Described in Simpson, 'The Bodleian Manuscripts of Henry King', *Bodleian Quarterly Record*, V, 339.

To Gilbert Sheldon, Archbishop of Canterbury, dated Aug. 16, 1668. Tanner MS., xliv, fol. 24. Described in Simpson, 'The Bodleian Manuscripts of Henry King', *Bodleian Quarterly Record*, V, 339.

To Mr More, n.d. Described in W. R. W. Stephens' *Diocesan Histories, the South Saxon Diocese, Selsey-Chichester* (London, 1881), pp. 226-27.

CRITICAL AND HISTORICAL WORKS

Andrewes, Lancelot, *Ninety-Six Sermons*, ed. J. P. Wilson, 5 vols. (Oxford, 1841-43).

Barton, William, *The Book of Psalms in Metre. Close and Proper to the Hebrew* (London, 1644).

Baxter, Richard, 'A Holy Commonwealth', *Richard Baxter and Puritan Politics*, ed. R. Schlatter (New Brunswick, 1957).

Berry, Francis, *Poets' Grammar* (London, 1958).

Bush, Douglas, *English Literature in the Earlier Seventeenth Century* (Oxford, 1962) second edn.

Butler, Samuel, *The Collected Works*, ed. A. R. Waller and R. Lamar, 3 vols. (Cambridge, England, 1905-28).

Castellio, Sebastian, *Concerning Heretics*, ed. R. Bainton (New York, 1935).

Cowley, Abraham, *The Essays and Other Prose Writings*, ed. A. B. Gough (Oxford, 1915).

Donne, John, *LXXX Sermons* (London, 1640).

——, *Essayes in Divinity* (London, 1651).

——, *The Poems of John Donne*, ed. Sir Herbert Grierson, 2 vols. (Oxford, 1912).

——, *The Sermons of John Donne*, ed. E. M. Simpson and G. R. Potter, 10 vols. (Berkeley, 1953-62).

Elson, James, *John Hales of Eton* (New York, 1948).

Filmer, Sir Robert, *Patriarcha: or the Natural Power of Kings* (London, 1680).

Foote, Henry, *Three Centuries of American Hymnody* (Cambridge, Mass., 1940).

Ford, Simon, *A New Version of the Psalms of David* (London, 1688).

Fox, George, *Journal*, ed. Thomas Ellwood (London, 1694).

Fuller, Thomas, *The Church History of Britain*, ed. J. S. Brewer, 6 vols. (Oxford, 1845).

——, *The Worthies of England*, ed. J. Freeman (London, 1952).

Gardiner, Samuel, *The Constitutional Documents of the Puritan Revolution* (Oxford, 1889).

Glanvill, Joseph, *Some Discourses, Sermons and Remains of the Reverend Mr. Jos. Glanvil* (London, 1681).

Gleckner, R. F., 'Henry King: A Poet of His Age', *Transactions of the Wisconsin Academy of Sciences, Arts and Letters*, XLV (1956), 149-67.

Gosse, Sir Edmund, *The Life and Letters of John Donne*, 2 vols. (New York, 1899).

Hales, John, *Works*, ed. D. Dalrymple, 3 vols. (Glasgow, 1765).

Haller, William, *The Rise of Puritanism* (New York, 1938).

Herbert, George, 'A Priest to the Temple', in *Works*, ed. F. E. Hutchinson (Oxford, 1941).

Holland, John, ed., *The Psalmists of Britain*, 2 vols. (London, 1843).

Hooker, Richard, *Of the Laws of Ecclesiastical Polity*, 2 vols. (London, 1907).

Howell, James, *Familiar Letters*, ed. J. Jacob, 2 vols. (London, 1890-92).

Hyde, Edward (Earl of Clarendon), *The History of the Rebellion and Civil Wars in England*, ed. W. D. MacRay, 6 vols. (Oxford, 1888).

James I, *The Political Works*, ed. C. H. McIlwain (Cambridge, Mass., 1918).

Jones, Richard F., *The Seventeenth Century* (Palo Alto, 1951).

Jonson, Ben, *Works*, ed. C. H. Herford, P. Simpson, and E. M. Simpson, 11 vols. (Oxford, 1925-52).

King, John, *The Fourth Sermon Preached at Hampton Court on Tuesday the last of Sept. 1606* (Oxford, 1606).

Mahood, M. M., *Poetry and Humanism* (London, 1950).

Martz, Louis, *The Poetry of Meditation* (New Haven, 1954).

Mason, Lawrence, 'The Life and Works of Henry King, D.D.', *Transactions of the Connecticut Academy of Arts and Sciences*, XVIII (November, 1913), 227-89.

Miles, Josephine, *The Continuity of Poetic Language* (Berkeley, 1951).

Mitchell, W. Fraser, *English Pulpit Oratory from Andrewes to Tillotson* (London, 1932).

'A Narration of the Burning of Bartholomew Legatt', *Truth brought to light and discovered by time, or a Discourse and Historicall Narration of the first XIIII yeares of King Iames Reigne* (London, 1651).

Niebuhr, Reinhold, *Faith and History* (New York, 1949).

Patrick, John, *Century of Select Psalms* (London, 1679).

Pepys, Samuel, *Diary*, ed. H. B. Wheatley, 10 vols. (London, 1893-99).

Prynne, William, *The Antipathie of the English Lordly Prelacie, Both to Regall Monarchy, and Civill Unity* (London, 1641).

Ryves, Bruno, *Mercurius Rusticus: or, The Countries Complaint of the Sacriledges, Prophanations, and Plunderings, Committed by the Schismatiques on the Cathedrall Churches of this Kingdome* (Oxford, 1646).

Simpson, Percy, 'The Bodleian Manuscripts of Henry King', *Bodleian Quarterly Record*, V (1926-28), 324-40.

——, 'John and Henry King: A Correction', *Bodleian Library Record*, IV (1952-53), 208-09.

South, Robert, *Sermons Preached Upon Severall Occasions*, 8 vols. (Oxford, 1842).

Spingarn, J. E., *Critical Essays of the Seventeenth Century*, 3 vols. (Oxford, 1908-09).

Stephens, W. R. W., *Diocesan Histories, the South Saxon Diocese, Selsey-Chichester* (London, 1881).

Stoughton, John, *Ecclesiastical History of England*, 5 vols. (London, 1867-74).

Sussex Archaeological Society, *Sussex Archaeological Collections* (London, 1848-1960).

Tillotson, John, *Sermons on Several Subjects and Occasions*, 11 vols. (London, 1742-44).

Tuve, Rosamund, *Elizabethan and Metaphysical Imagery* (Chicago, 1947).

Von Rohr-Sauer, Philip, *English Metrical Psalms from 1600-1660* (Freiburg, 1938).

Walker, John, *An Attempt Towards Recovering an Account of the Numbers and Sufferings of the Clergy of the Church of England* (London, 1714).

Wallerstein, Ruth, *Studies in Seventeenth-Century Poetic* (Madison, Wis., 1950).

Walton, Izaak, *The Life of John Donne* (London, 1658).

——, *Lives* (Oxford, 1927).

——, *The Compleat Walton*, ed. Geoffrey Keynes (London, 1929).

Wood, Anthony à, *Athenae Oxoniensis*, ed. P. Bliss, 4 vols. (London, 1813-20).

Woodford, Samuel, *A Paraphrase Upon the Psalms of David* (London, 1667).

INDEX